THE POWER OF A WHISPER

My Unexpected Journey
and the Everyday Wisdom It Holds

DR. ROD CASEY

Carriage
House
PUBLISHERS

Published by
Carriage House Publishers
Library of Congress Control Number: 2025925835
Paperback ISBN: 979-8-9925086-2-8
Cover and Interior Design: Carolyn Preul
Copy Editor: Sandy Selby
Printed in the United States of America

To the next generation of ministry leaders,
especially Silas, Lydia, Lucy, and Oliver.

Thank you for the privilege of investing in you.

I love you.

Endorsements

"It is a gift to read a collection of one's life who has lived in sold-out obedience to God. Even though I have heard many of these stories while sitting across from the man himself, I am eager to read the thought-out and revised versions of these moments. Spending one hour with Rod is always a gift, so having a book filled with his words-what could we call that? Wisdom tied with tenderness is what you should expect from this book, and it is something I often find absent in the ministry world today. I am excited to read about how God's voice still guides us presently in the crossroads moments of our lives."   — ELLIOT MUHLENBRUCK

* * *

"*The Power of a Whisper* invites readers to pay attention to the quiet but powerful ways God meets us in everyday life. Rod has been a mentor and spiritual father to me, so reading this feels like being invited back into the conversations that have shaped my life. Rod shares his journey with honesty and openness, and that makes the stories easy to connect with. He doesn't gloss over the disappointments or struggles but instead shows how God's whispers can guide us through them. The mix of real-life experiences and Spirit led reflection makes this book both practical and encouraging. Anyone who reads it will be stirred to notice the Spirit's voice in their own story and to step out with fresh courage."

— JEREMY PATTY

* * *

"Since I was a teen, I've had the privilege of sitting with Rod at a Panera or a HyVee cafe, learning from his battle tested wisdom. Most of his lessons included drawings he made with a Uniball pen on the back of a napkin. During my own two decades of working in pastoral ministry, I've wished to have a reference book filled with all those napkins and lessons. *The Power of a Whisper* is that text. Not many days pass that his shared knowledge doesn't inform my own decision making. In Rod's distinctive style, he tackles often-overlooked aspects of pastoral leadership. He effectively teaches from his own experiences about the ways the Holy Spirit speaks, leads, cares for, and guards those He loves. All of this he shares in tenderness and deep affection for the next generation of leaders in the Church. This resource is a master's degree in listening and, even more importantly, resting in the gift that is the Holy Spirit."

— GRANT ARMSTRONG

* * *

"Rod Casey's work reminds us that God often moves in the midst of the mundane. With honesty and humility, he shares personal yet relatable stories, showing how a simple nudge from the Spirit can change everything if we are willing to listen. Rod's gift for mentoring also comes through on the page in the way he asks questions that draw the reader into reflection. His writing carries the same wisdom and encouragement I have experienced from him personally in moments when I needed a listening ear."

— DAVID NONNENMACHER JR.

* * *

"The content of this book, stories of Rod's life journey and his reflections, are both edifying and affirming. Rod affirms the significance of challenges and burdens I'm facing by sharing his experiences. I have also faced many of the challenges he describes here. He and I have personally discussed these as well. But there are so many battles I have not yet fought. His experience and resulting wisdom are everything I could hope for as a young Christian called to lead others. I am honored to be among the first to receive sections of this book, and to have Rod as a personal mentor in my journey as a man seeking to do well as a servant of the Lord and a leader to my fellow Christ followers."   — TONY VOELLER

* * *

"God doesn't care what color car you buy or whether you purchase this house or that!" I've repeated this time and again over the course of two decades of ministry. And yet, as followers of Jesus, we understand that the Spirit does speak to us if we are willing to listen, even in the seemingly mundane details of life. The degree and magnitude depend on our willingness to listen and submit to His direction. In *The Power of a Whisper*, Dr. Rod Casey recounts his own real-world experiences of following the prompting of the Spirit through various seasons of his life. This book, with its practical and applicable guidance, will serve as a tool for hearing and heeding the Holy Spirit in everyday life, in decisions that seem inconsequential and those that will impact the world."

— JOSEPH LANHAM

* * *

"As a developing church planter and ministry leader, I often find myself praying for wisdom. *The Power of a Whisper* is an answer to that prayer. In this practical memoir, Rod traces his faith journey and ministry path with a refreshing honesty and vulnerability, offering the next generation of leaders an uncommon window into the realities of ministry along with opportunities for reflection. He invites readers into a series of note-worthy Spirit interruptions in his own life that led to paradigm shifts. Extending beyond his personal story, these lessons now serve as helpful guideposts for the next generation of leaders, helping us to avoid the pitfalls of striving, burnout, and neglect of a tender, Christ-centered heart."

— MEGHAN BISHOP

* * *

"I've served in full time ministry for more than two decades, and Rod has consistently been a tremendous source of encouragement. He's helped me navigate the kinds of obstacles that often sideline ministry leaders. I'm thrilled that he has poured his wisdom and experience into this book, so that others can receive the same life-giving impact I have. This resource will be a catalyst for longevity and fruitfulness for anyone who picks it up."

— LUKE NEAL

* * *

"Rod Casey has been a faithful mentor and guide to countless ministry leaders, myself included. In *The Power of a Whisper*, he draws from his decades of experience to help readers learn how to recognize and respond to the Spirit's leading in both ordinary and unexpected moments. His honesty about the challenges of ministry, combined with the wisdom of lived experience, makes this book both relatable and deeply encouraging to every person of faith. I believe this resource will bless the next generation of leaders who want to grow in discernment, courage, and faith. Anyone longing to follow Jesus with greater attentiveness will find hope and direction in these pages."

— NEAL BENSON

* * *

"Rod has shaped my growth in Jesus by modeling how to listen to the Holy Spirit and use my gifts to join in what Jesus is doing around me. His story carries the kind of authenticity and hope that can only come from a life lived attentive to God's voice. This book reflects both the wisdom of experience and the courage of faith. It will serve as a valuable resource for next-generation leaders seeking to navigate their calling with clarity and purpose."   — MONICA MILLER BROWN

* * *

"This book will be a great encouragement and help to servants of Christ's kingdom. Rod Casey's wisdom and wit are both on full display here as he reflects on lessons learned through years of experience, refined by many fires. These pages are theologically rich and eminently practical. God has already used Rod to bless so many, including me, and this book represents the culmination of his impact."   — JESSE BINGHAM

* * *

"Knowing Rod and the way he has poured into people over the years, I have no doubt that this book will be full of the same wisdom, humility, and Spirit-led insight he brings to every conversation. His life and ministry have impacted so many, and I'm excited to see that same heart for mentoring and spiritual formation now shared in written form. Truly a great resource for the next generation of ministry leaders."

— AIDEN LOCKETT

* * *

"Dr. Rod has been the mentor to me that I wish I had (more of). This vulnerable account of his 'wasted-years-discipleship' is a precious gift to me as I navigate my own confusing seasons. Dr. Rod's conversational tone and his "teaching through story" approach make this book accessible and alluring. I can't wait to see how God uses this work to disciple the lives of us younger bucks who are in the middle of it!"   — PETE KEIZER

* * *

"Rod's ministry and mentorship have been a profound gift to me. Only a vibrant walk with the Spirit can sustain us when life 'kicks the snot out of us.' Rod demonstrates just such a walk. I pray *The Power of a Whisper* will be a gift to you as well." — MICHAEL KAUFFMAN

* * *

"There are times when the paths lined out by those who are further ahead of us in ministry start to fade and we find ourselves in a field with no clear direction. It's in those seasons that a guide is imperative to continued advancement and long-term flourishing. Rod has been such a guide in many lives and situations and it's a privilege to have his wisdom and life experience in this book. I'm looking forward to further gleaning from the real-life accounts of transition, the unexpected, and the fruit to following Christ closely with no regrets. I'm confident that all who read this book will not only read about the 'power of a whisper' but will also experience such power through the heartfelt pages of wisdom from preface to appendix." — D'MARKUS THOMAS-BROWN

* * *

"God delighted to express Himself 'in the flesh' through Christ Jesus. Our everyday needs are met in His incarnation as we tangibly share in experiencing Him among the 'one another's.' Rod captures his life experiences of this reality so well, providing a roadmap for readers to apply in their own lives. I've personally grown from Christ in Rod's story for years. Enjoy Jesus among us in this helpful resource, you won't regret it!" — SCOTT CLAYBROOK

* * *

"As people in the 'you're not old enough to be great yet' and 'you are the curriculum' stage of life, we've been deeply shaped by Rod's wisdom and mentorship over the past decade. His insights come from walking closely with the Holy Spirit through both successes and failures, and his willingness to share these stories has helped us discern God's work in our own lives. In this book, Rod recounts those same lessons and reflections, making his guidance accessible to anyone seeking to grow in faith and leadership. You don't want to miss it!"

— ELIZABETH AND ZANE CLARK

Foreword

These stories are my spiritual heritage. Many of them are like a soundtrack I've heard over the course of my life. A few of them I witnessed first-hand, privy to the wrestling and mining for God's goodness in the middle of things. In all of them, my dad has always and only pointed me back to the Author of the stories, the One in whom all our stories are found whole and full of true life. My faith is bolstered because of them!

As a next generation ministry leader, these accounts take on added layers of meaning. The treasures in this book offer both invitation and challenge to lead from a depth of trust in God's voice first and foremost, which open us up to greater humility, care, and intentionality in leading God's people. These stories keep shaping the ways that I hear and respond to God as I steward my influence.

I have witnessed the pain of ministry peers and friends whose seasoned leaders and parents in their midst have been critical because of the ways that a next-gen leader is wrestling deeply with faithful witness to Jesus in this complex cultural moment. That is not what my dad has offered me, and I know that is a precious gift. In the strongest of terms, my dad has both affirmed and commissioned in word and empowering action to faithfully follow Jesus into my Kingdom calling. He has released me to wrestle with God, ask challenging questions, experiment with new ways of ministry, and even receive my leadership.

It is a joy to know that I am not the only one who receives this kind of empowerment from him. He journeys with so many of us in curiosity, not criticism. Wisdom and hope, not narrow methods. Stories, not shoulds. We don't need more hot takes about the right way to think and lead. We need men and women, like my dad, who know intimately the kindness of God, the love of Jesus, and the power of the Spirit. We need the courageous articulation of a real life with God, in all of its beauty and struggle, hope and uncertainty. That is what we are offered in these pages.

Our world is in desperate need of local faith communities who bear witness to Jesus, in their words and their works. Those of us called to lead these communities need all the wisdom we can get. We need to embrace humility by deep learning from our own stories and the stories of ones who have gone before us. *The Power of a Whisper* extends a hand to us for that end.

To the next gen leaders—may we let this book prod us to stay with Jesus, to keep adventuring with God, to welcome the whispers of the Spirit, and to deepen our hope in God's good, redemptive work over the course of our lives.

To the mentors—may you let this book prod you to stay with Jesus, to help you mine your own stories of God's redemptive work in your life, to embrace growing and learning no matter your age, and deepen your gratitude in God's renewal over the course of your life.

To all of us—may we allow this book to attune our hearts to the whispers from The One who is transforming all things for our good, and for the good of the world.

— Miriam J. (Casey) Knight

THE POWER
OF A WHISPER

Contents

———

* * *

My hopes of becoming a music teacher were dashed. What was I going to major in now? My life's calling was just a semester away.

I was settling into the Dallas Seminary model when I was accosted by the Holy Spirit's question. I'm still a little ticked off about the way my plan for ministry success was interrupted.

There ought to be a church for a guy like Rick to go to. Meeting an unreached adult at church was unexpected. His candid comments changed the trajectory of my life.

Infertility is hard on a couple who long for a child. I didn't want to add to my wife's grief by telling her what I heard the Spirit telling me to tell her.

The church plant wasn't sustainable. I needed employment. I knew what I needed to do, but I couldn't without being disobedient to an unexpected whisper.

* * *

Often life is lived in obedience while heaven seems silent. Here I describe
a season when we "hit a wall." In times like these, it's doing what we know
and holding out for "daily bread" that sees us through.

A spiritual practice for inviting the Holy Spirit's promptings and leadings.

Preface

——

I F MY INTENTIONS FOR this resource are realized, the reader will see God as the hero. Our life stories matter because God has a Story. We are invited to cooperate with Him as we create our own stories and make ourselves helpful to others and their stories.

What you hold in your hands is an account of some of my stories. These stories have a convergence. If you're unfamiliar with the term, think of it as the collection of several streams, including family background, education, wounds, victories, mentors, passions, and God-moments. Each flows separately for a while, but eventually they come together with the potential to form a powerful current with direction and momentum. My convergence is mentoring the next generation of leaders, particularly those involved in ministry endeavors. Few things bring me greater joy. I'm telling these stories to tell God's story. In telling my stories, I'm hoping to persuade future generations to pay attention to the power of His whispers and bet on God to give them an unexpected, yet flourishing life.

In this book, you'll find large swaths of my spiritual journey. Along the way, you may be tempted to label me charismatic. However, little about me would suggest a flair for charisma. Not personality.

Not practice. Nada. I rarely lift one hand during a praise set. On occasion, two hands if it's palms up and only waist high. I've never spoken in tongues. I've never prayed for someone's healing and seen it happen on the spot. I visited Bethel Church once when I was in Redding while teaching an intensive week at Tozer Seminary ... and still nothing. I sat through two "Toronto Blessing" (holy laughter) breakouts here in Columbia, Missouri, and never gave up so much as a chuckle.

Labels that are more fitting for my tribal history would include independent Baptist, dispensational premillennialist, mega-church/seeker movement, and a Billy Graham evangelical. But not charismatic. That's why this writing seems weird coming from me. It's why I'm a little reluctant to share it.

In each of the 12 chapters, there are unexpected encounters I've had with the Spirit's voice. I trust you'll come to grasp the way I'm using the word "unexpected." It's kind of like the Daisy brand BB gun I got for Christmas when I was a boy. It really opened new adventures in the woods behind our house, but you could also put an eye out with it. Or kill a bluebird, which made Mom cry. Hearing the Holy Spirit's voice is a resource with power that leads us in our faith adventures.

Perhaps that's a part of the outcome intended. God leads each of us in unique ways, and often in ways that are not the ones we'd choose, but exactly the ones we need. I'm convinced one size doesn't fit all when it comes to personal revelation.

If my mentor hadn't expressed an openness to it, I don't think I would have been open to experiencing supernatural instruction. To be more accurate I wouldn't have named it. I had experienced it already, as you'll read about it in the first chapter, but in the theological academy I was being trained in, we didn't admit it. Nor did we talk about it. Not really.

I attended Dallas Theological Seminary when the charisma hit the fan.[1] Three professors lost their jobs around 1987, the same year I graduated with a Th.M. (master's in theology) degree. What conviction got them in doctrinal hot water? Their sympathies with charismatic theology. Jack Deere was my Hebrew professor, and he got "Surprised by the Spirit."[2]

Walter Bodine taught my Old Testament Intro course and he spent the first half of each class telling us about his healing from emotional pain when John Wimber laid hands on him and prayed. I didn't mind. It was better than learning why higher criticism was flawed and why we could trust that Moses through oral tradition was the original author. Wouldn't you rather hear about present-day divine activity than learn that? Point made.

My major was pastoral ministries, and homiletics (preaching) was my emphasis. Don Sunukjian had my attention both in and out of the classroom. When Don was hired in 1979, he was clear in his contention that it could not be proven biblically that these gifts (tongues and healing) were limited to New Testament times. His study break during my third year (of four) included the Fuller Seminary Institute of Church Growth. During our final year, he shared with us in class his curiosity regarding the principles that organization was suggesting.

---

1   *Three Professors Part Paths with Dallas.* Christianity Today magazine. February 5, 1988. Vol. 32, no. 2.

2   Deere, Jack. *Surprised by the Power of the Holy Spirit.* Grand Rapids: Zondervan Academic, 1996. 302 p.

As if that weren't enough exposure, the Dallas area church we attended, named "Metropolitan Tabernacle," was historically Oneness Pentecostal. Though Pastor Charles Diffee (the founding pastor's son) had led the church into an evangelical/orthodox doctrinal position, the congregation had a compelling kindness about them grounded in an appreciation for the better parts of their Spirit-filled heritage.

All that is to say, I'm grateful for the providential season we were unexpectedly exposed to during our time in Dallas. It gave me a willingness to "hear" the Spirit's voice and now share some of those experiences with you.

In the first ten chapters, you will read about direct encounters. Those were times when a thought I had that I knew wasn't my thought came directly into my mind, or soul, or spirit, or whatever you want to call it. I heard it directly.

The final two chapters discuss indirect encounters. I write about experiences where a physical person said something, but I heard it so profoundly that I knew immediately that a divine voice was giving me profound personal revelation. I'm confident the reader will identify with these experiences more readily. They are common among believers willing to admit them. Scripture, praise songs, the counsel of a trusted friend, even circumstances communicate God's heart for us personally as we navigate what it means to live life as an apprentice of Jesus, submitted to the Father, through the presence of the Holy Spirit.

At the end of each telling of an unexpected encounter, I imagine a response you as the reader may be having and will attempt to share wise counsel regarding your own life. I also include next steps you might take if you resonate with the help offered.

In the afterword, you will read about my most recent silent encounter: a "Wall" as Peter Scazzero writes about it when he quotes from ancient spiritual mothers and fathers in the faith regarding the dark night of the soul.[3] In these experiences, we trust in God's person and promises, even when His presence eludes us. I think it essential to include this spiritual reality in a book like this, and I implore you to not skip it. In fact, I strongly encourage you to read it first.

Keeping the faith with you,
rod

---

3   Scazzero, Pete. *Emotionally Healthy Spirituality*. Zondervan, Grand Rapids: 2017, updated edition, pp. 97-116.

CHAPTER ONE

"Take a professor."

—

" **T**HE FACULTY LIKE YOU very much," Mrs. Regina Brown said kindly, "but the answer is no." The question being answered was whether the music faculty of the Christian college I was attending, Tennessee Temple University, would let me minor in music so that I could pursue a vocation in music education.

"But the answer is no." These words shouted in my head repeatedly as I made my way across campus, opened the heavy door of Phillips Dorm, and rolled into the bottom bed of the bunk. Once settled, the loud refrain of their rejection made their way from my head down into my soul and back up again into inconsolable sobs.

Having cried myself out, I then did what young believers are prone to do in their immature despair: I threw open the approved translation of that faith tradition, the King James Bible, put my finger on a verse and started reading. As God is gracious to do, Heavenly Father met me in those verses despite my interpretive misconceptions, and soon I found devotional application sufficient to get me out of bed with hope for a meaningful future.

Looking back, I didn't really like music—not like I know people now who do. Nor was I all that good at it. I had begged my mom to let me quit piano lessons after just a few months. I played the coronet (a small trumpet) in the middle school band but dropped out when I left middle school. Our church had a youth choir that I think I joined, though I may not have had a choice. I can't remember. Given my compliant nature and introvert personality that longed for friends, I didn't dislike going and was told that I had a good singing voice.

Beyond choir, when invited I used that voice to sing what was called a "special" during a church service. The "special" was the song the congregation didn't participate in that happened just before the "main event" when the pastor gave the sermon. The "special" music may be a choir, or duet or trio, but often it was a solo. And from time to time, I sang that solo.

"I must tell Jesus all of my trials. I cannot bear these burdens alone. In my distress he kindly will help me. He ever loves and cares for His own. I must tell Jesus! I must tell Jesus. I cannot bear these burdens alone. I must tell Jesus. I must tell Jesus. Jesus can help me. Jesus alone!" This is one of the songs I remember singing to a crowd of several hundred attendees. Hand clapping was off limits but as the last note faded, a hearty "amen" was affirming as I stepped away from the pulpit.

Implicitly, I had three motivations for thinking that music was my future as I headed off to college. First, my mom loved music, and I loved my mom. Though embarrassed, I usually accommodated her request to perform when visiting her relatives in nearby states. "Sing for Aunt Nell and Aunt Grace that "special" you sang at church last Sunday night. You know, 'Savior, Like a Shepherd Lead Us' isn't it called? Just the first verse and chorus. Please, Rodney? I know they'll love it."

A second thing motivating a future in music was getting my father's attention. Looking back, I'm certain that an implicit reason for my musical ambition was every young man's longing for his father's blessing.

My workaholic pastor/father loved his vocation, and it came at the cost of a relationship with me. My default memory of him is the back of his head as he entered the back door of the church while I bounced a basketball to myself and wished he would stop and play for a minute. What did catch his gaze was when I led the music for younger children after a week of church camp or sang the "special" before the sermon he preached. A hearty "amen" from him after it concluded was a healing salve to my aching soul. "Am I enough?" is every boy's question. I like to think my dad saw me as having a future edifying God's people, even though my contribution has been homiletical instead of musical.

And finally, I was motivated musically because I did indeed want to invite others to experience life in the kingdom of Jesus as I had been invited. The lyrics of a song gave to me the words at a time I was lacking my own. Through music I could communicate that life goes better with Jesus in it. I bet my life on that idea and music was an age-appropriate way for me to participate.

With my college plans thwarted, I spent the early part of that summer wondering what my sophomore course schedule might include. One day, I had a thought that I knew was not my thought. It was more like a whisper. But this whisper had power. Power enough to draw my attention to it and power enough to keep my attention. In short, I couldn't forget it. I now know that "it" was the "Spir-it" and the proposition is a person. The power of that whisper is a benefit of our new life in Christ, and the focus of this collection of stories from my life journey.

The thought that was whispered to my soul was this: "**Take a professor instead of a class.**" I had never thought this thought before. I'm confident I had never heard anyone else suggest it, though it is wisdom I share with students heading off for their own undergraduate studies. "Consider what kind of person you want to become as much or more than the vocation you'd like to pursue." That's the contribution I offer from my experience in this regard.

When the registrar's office posted the upcoming class schedule for the fall on the bulletin board outside the office (that's right, a hard copy printout before the days of digital access), because of the whisper's power, I turned my gaze first to the teacher column instead of the class title. There I saw the name Dennis Michelson and then the course title, Homiletics. I signed up because of *the power of that whisper*.

I didn't know it was the study of preaching. Homiletics is from the root word "homily," an ancient Greek word referring to a crowd or assembly for a conversation or a discourse. That fall I was sitting in a class being introduced to rhetorical resources available for preaching. When applied, these communication tools increase the chances that the assertion made by the communicator will enhance clarity and relevance for the listeners, and that something in the congregants' world will be different because they acted upon it.

Without question, homiletics was the first accredited class I ever took that I loved; I learned the content without even trying. I had heard others describe this phenomenon, but it wasn't until my sophomore year of undergrad that I found my academic home.

I enjoyed learning and had been an avid reader of frontier and missionary biographies in my primary years. Later, nonfiction resources from Twin City Christian Bookstore where I was employed during my adolescence had whetted my appetite for ministry. But this field of study for me was different. It energized and motivated me in the classroom like basketball did out of the classroom. You didn't have to ask me if I wanted to practice or play; I couldn't wait to do so.

I do recall Dr. Michelson correcting my (mis)pronunciation of the name King Darius after one of my classroom sermons. I now know there's no way of knowing how ancient languages sounded out, only what is culturally acceptable. As a result, I encourage my students that when pronouncing difficult Bible words, to say them with confidence since no one really knows. Quoting a high school basketball coach, "A little bit of hustle makes up for a whole lot of mistakes."

It was while reading the course textbook, "Preaching and Preachers" by D. Martyn Lloyd-Jones, that I embraced my ministry calling. In it, the author describes five things ministry leaders who are "called" typically experience. They are: 1. want to (desire), 2. can't quit thinking about it (time), 3. maturer people saying you should consider it (elders), 4. the Holy Spirit's whisper, and 5. you're pretty good at it (affirmation) or care about it when you experience it being done poorly (holy discontent). I was five for five and simply bowed my head in the university library after reading his criteria and said "yes."

After my first easy A, I changed my major to Christian Ministries. It was educational philosophy applied to faith life courses combined with some required Bible classes. It was perfect for me and for my life's work. Providential. Wouldn't you agree? And what was my part? To grieve the gift of a music faculty's rejection (brutal) and receive the whisper of a Holy Spirit who knew me better than I knew myself and knew God had a wonderful plan for my life (beautiful). My wife and I have a word for that... *breautiful.*

YOUR STORY

As you read my story, I'm wondering what closed doors you are experiencing. It is so hard to keep the faith when circumstances beyond your control happen. Betting on God is tough when you go for broke and run into a brick wall. Perhaps the girl you thought you would grow old with suddenly broke up with a text. It said, "Hey. Feelings have changed, and it seems that the relationship won't work out. The memories made will be cherished, but it's time to move on. Hope you understand." What makes it worse is that your dad liked her so much he whispered to you while celebrating your niece's birthday, "Don't screw this up. She's a keeper." I know you keep obsessing over what you could have done differently. You feel gutted.

Or perhaps you are a woman who wants to learn how to preach, but the seminary you attend holds a traditional view. The camaraderie the guys share in the student center after class galls you for good reason. You want to proclaim the ageless wisdom of Scripture in culturally relevant language for your generation. Some of your professors and male peers confess they are "closet mutualists," but what can they do, they tell you. The door to take a preaching course is closed.

Both real life situations above and more are the stuff that living is made of. Ugh is a word I use when I don't know what else to say. Ugh to a closed door. Ugh to a shattered hope. Ugh! But please don't give up or give in. Please keep the faith. Learn the dance moves to Forrest Frank's "Your Ways Better" and bet on God to put your heart back together. Like Toby Mac said, "When life cuts so deep, try and remember ... scars come with livin'!"

This might be helpful. I've found that I imagined my future in very specific terms. For example, when I was younger, I could only find meaning if my future included teaching in a traditional bible college or seminary. Or I wrongly believed ministry could only be done in a formal church setting. Or I had to be the lead pastor who taught weekly, or I wouldn't be satisfied.

What I now realize is that my life-giving contributions are not confined to a particular setting. In fact, those specific spaces are too limiting. My younger self experiences helped define the spaces that fit better. I did ministry when I was employed at McDonald's. I couldn't help but discuss the problem of evil with Cordell as we were breaking down boxes to put in the recycling bin. Adjunct teaching scratched my itch to participate in higher education without the administrative department meetings or accreditation reports that came with full-time employment.

And when the door closed on our church plant endeavor, I was elated to be relieved from the weekly preparation of giving the sermon. It wasn't me. I liked studying what I wanted to instead and contributing to the mid-week discipleship environments instead. I don't teach in a formal seminary, but the theological education initiative (a nonprofit answer to the lack of one in our community) is about as close as you can get.

Your experiences, including the disappointing ones, help you know who you are or what you do and don't want to do. Don't shrink back from changing your major. Don't get trapped in a job because it will look good on your resume. Give yourself permission to change your mind, even if a parent or peers don't approve. Reflect deeply and ask, "Jesus, what do you and I want to do?" Ask Him for a thought not your own. If the Spirit has something to say, it will get said. If not, bet on God. Do what you-in-Jesus, Jesus-in-you want to do.

1. What closed door(s) have you encountered that you are grieving?
2. What barrier(s) are keeping you from pursuing a God-in-you longing?
3. Discuss with friends what Luke, Paul, and Silas might have felt as they encountered conflict with Barnabas, an open door to Asia Minor, and the surprise of finding Lydia and her friends waiting for their good news. (Acts 15:36-16:15)
4. Journal a prayer to God about a closed door that you are hurting from and ask Him for strength to still bet your future on Him.

CHAPTER TWO

"Are you going to give the rest of your life to this?"

———

AFRIEND AND I rebelled in college. We started listening to Moody Bible Radio Network. Yep! That's right. I was a late bloomer when it came to sneaking around doing something I shouldn't have been doing. While many teens start experimenting with things the adults around them say are dangerous and should be avoided, I didn't take that kind of risk until my last two years of college.

I was a "good kid" growing up—compliant and spiritually inclined. I've been told repeatedly that wisdom, simply defined, is the art of living life skillfully. It is a recurring spiritual gift that those around me benefit from. No wonder perhaps, I have a Bible from my pre-teen years where I wrote in the flyleaf, "God, give me wisdom." I overheard older people I respected say of me, "He's wise beyond his years." This set the bar high, and I was motivated to meet it.

In addition, baked into the DNA of my childhood theology was a "God will like you more" if you didn't go to the movies, kept your hair off your ears (guys), didn't wear pants (girls), had daily devotions (two chapters), attended all three services (plus Sunday School and Training Union), went soul winning, only Christian cussed (for heaven's sake), didn't play basketball on Sunday, and "didn't smoke or chew or go with the girls who do." In short, I drank the Kool-Aid, theologically speaking. I bet on God, the advice of authority figures around me, and walked the straight and narrow until the day a college friend introduced me to a drug called "grace" and it came in the form of radio waves from a dealer in Chicago.

Tennessee Temple University landed somewhere between Bob Jones and Liberty Universities, if you know what that means. It wasn't as strict as it could have been, but it didn't allow music with a rock 'n' roll beat or dating off-campus without a chaperone. You got demerits for missing curfew or chapel. Christian service was required and reported on. I reflect on it now as a ministry boot camp of sorts. Many great memories, tons of delightful people, and enough "works-based" discipleship to take a lifetime to get over. That's where the rebellious step I finally took comes into play.

Moody Bible Radio was off-limits on our campus, or at least it was implicitly implied if not explicitly communicated. The university had its own station (WDYN) and radio preachers that were approved and promoted. I was about to experiment with discipleship elements not found on that approved list.

Rocky Gill was "dealing grace" just outside the lobby of Phillips Dorm. He introduced me to a "a station broadcasting out of Atlanta with the preaching of Charles Stanley and Chuck Swindoll." The contemporary sounds of Sandi Patty and Larnell Harris singing syncopated non-hymns were also a part of the trip.

Dr. Stanley's teaching on the "exchanged life" wasn't brand new for me. I'd heard Jim Hylton encourage this Keswick brand of sanctification (how we mature in Christ) when I was a boy. My home church splashed around in the shallow end of "works-based" discipleship, but TTU had me swimming in the deep end. Could it be possible that God liked me and didn't scowl when I didn't want to go soul winning or street preaching in downtown Chattanooga anymore?

In short, Keswick theology teaches that the antidote to sin management for the believer is to know their identity in Christ and live confident that "He who began a good work in you will be faithful to complete it." (Phil. 1:6) This teaching does not teach the eradication of sin, yet the believer only has one nature with coping mechanisms (Romans 7) that are being renewed day by day. Our union with Christ is the truest thing about us and sin occurs when we forget who we are. What if God isn't mad at you? What if God really likes you, even on your worst day?

While the exchanged life teaching was revolutionary, it was the "Insight for Living" broadcast that rocked my world even more. Charles Swindoll had me at "Call me Chuck." His accessible personality, his down-home humor, his knowledge of the Scriptures combined with his culturally connected illustrations and real-life applications left me feeling better than making a hook shot from outside the lane to win a basketball game.

When my mother asked me what I wanted as a gift for graduation from college, my answer was immediate: "I want to take a trip to visit a school in Dallas."

"What school is it and why?" she asked.

"I don't know anything about it," I answered. "All I know is that it's where this guy on the radio went and I want to learn the Bible like he knows it and learn how to communicate it half as well!" I replied. Given her Texas roots and the opportunity to visit family while there, she agreed to come with me to Texas. I applied to that school and began my graduate studies a year later.

My time at Dallas Theological Seminary was all and more than I hoped for. Howard Hendricks inspired me. Norm Geisler engaged my doubts. Don Sunukjian taught me how to preach like Chuck did. And John Martin walked me through the 66 books of the Bible (a DTS distinction). I loved my DTS experience.

Instead of attending Scofield Memorial Church or Rheinhardt Bible like many DTS students did, my wife, Julie, and I found a home at Metropolitan Bible Church on Bruton Road. This faith community and its pastors, including Pastor Charles and Mrs. Diffee, welcomed us warmly and invited us to participate. Julie was employed in the church office, and I was hired as an intern.

I was in my final year of studies when I was accosted by another unexpected whisper. Our staff meeting concluded and I was excited to be included in the discussion. Our agenda that day took up the entire meeting: Should we change the starting time of the adult education/Sunday School program from 9:30 to 9:45 am in the hope that an additional 30 people would come? I don't remember my perspective, but the prospect of teaching what I was learning in seminary to more people had my attention.

When I returned to my broom closet-sized office, I sat back in my chair to gather myself, I experienced a thought that wasn't my thought challenging my cessationist, charismatic-free, rational-laden reality. **"Are you going to give the rest of your life to this?"** the Whisper asked.

"Duh, yes!" was my default response. "Of course, I am. That's why I walked away from the blessing of my home church and risked disappointing some members of my family. I made sacrifices to attend a seminary that didn't fly an independent Baptist flag and hitched my wagon to the Bible church movement. This is what we do. We take what we learned in the classroom and redistribute it to our congregations," I continued indignantly. "My past was about evangelism and discipleship lite. My future is about expositional teaching and knowledge driven spiritual formation. I'm going to accept a call, sit on an all-male elder board, preach on Sundays, and pastor people during the week." I wasn't quite done when I concluded, "They'll give me a salary. I'll get a doctorate. And maybe someday I'll teach in a Bible college or seminary, here or overseas, all the wonderful things that have been invested in me." That's what I told the Holy Whisper in no uncertain terms.

Where the Holy Spirit took me next disrupted the plans I had for the future … big time. In some ways, I find myself still reeling emotionally from the paradigm hijack described above. But following is Jesus is like that, isn't it?! Unexpected. Uneasy. Unsettling. Unpredictable. And that makes for better stories.

"Do you know ten people outside of your Christian bubble?" the thoughts in my spiritual mind said. "Do you know five? One?" I remembered the woman living in the apartment under ours and wondered if she were facing a Christless eternity. I hadn't ever given it a thought until then.

Four years attending a Christian high school. Four more years in a Christian college. Four more years in a theological seminary hadn't left much room for giving a hoot about those unaware of the benefits of an abundant life in Jesus. Justifiably I thought,

I had knocked on doors in high school, helped with an after-noon Sunday School to disadvantaged kids in college, and we befriended Korean immigrants who managed the laundromat near our apartment. We'd even spent a summer in Korea and in the Philippine islands visiting missionaries and contemplating missionary service overseas. I gave mental assent to the need to share our faith with others. I'd taken a course in evangelism from Dr. Tony Evans. I'd been greatly impacted by Joe Aldrich's book, "Lifestyle Evangelism." I just didn't ever decide to prioritize it or do it. I wanted to preach and teach and motivate others to do it after they learned what I'd learned, knew what I knew, theologi-cally speaking.

Something shifted after that experience. I saw with new eyes women and men outside that bubble, and a passion began to grow for seeing adults who were far from God become fully devoted to God. I stopped misbelieving that if we just "one-another-ed" each other enough we'd somehow mysteriously self-combust into a movement so powerful that non-Christians would flock to our churches wanting to know what is going on in there.

I began to see the New Testament concept known as "people of peace," as the author Luke records concerning the Centurion (Luke 7), the Ethiopian (Acts 8), and Lydia (Acts 16). The idea of staying alert to people, being hospitable or easy to talk to as people prepared by God to share the gospel with was a far cry from accosting unsuspecting individuals in the grocery parking lot asking if they knew where they'd go if they died tonight.

I was helped significantly by the writing of missiologist David Hesselgrave in his book, "Planting Churches Cross-Culturally: North America and Beyond." He taught me the concept known as contextualization. Contextualization is the work of communicating the ageless truths of God's revelation in the language of a people group's culture. Using their heart language instead of your own preferred language. Not with the intent of making the message palatable, but understandable and applied in every context.

Plowing, persuading, sowing, serving, being less weird, taking relational risks, and asking better questions when dialoguing with seekers ... all these and more were a part of the seismic shift that happened the day I heard Someone whisper, "Are you going to give the rest of your life to this?"

This new passion for reaching the unchurched and discipling them to maturity was making sense of the journey thus far. The evangelistic passion of my adolescence combined with the discipleship commitment I was learning at DTS need not be bifurcated. It's not either/or, it's both/and. This new insight was soon to be affirmed and tested.

YOUR STORY

I'm wondering about your story. Where did you grow up? How did your parents talk about God and such? Where are you in the birth order? Did your mom divorce the "sperm donor" as she called your dad or vice versa? Are you an avid indoorsman with passive inclinations or a manly man with Incredible Hulk tendencies? Do you resist talking about it? What parts do you not want to share? And what do these questions have to do with the confusing season you are currently experiencing when it feels like you are wasting your life?

I get it. I've often said that the hardest part of pastoral ministry is processing me. What older me knows now that I wish younger me had known then is that the curriculum is me. During the season you just read about, I was focused on the outcomes of what I was going to do. The product involved where I would work, what title and role I would have, and what organizations I would belong to. Would I be great? These questions and more were the front and center of my attention.

But in retrospect, I now see that the questions God was asking (if you can let me put it that way for a minute) were more like this: What does Rod need in order to fulfill his kingdom assignments and finish them with a heart tender toward Me (God), himself, and others? Can you see it? I was too young to be great. My 20s and 30s weren't the end game. I needed preparation to maximize my future contribution and so do you. While that's still true of me, it was especially true early on.

Put differently, nothing gets wasted in God's kingdom economy. The twists and turns leave us feeling spiritually whiplashed. "But God, I thought we were going this way. But now, what are we doing? But God, these are my people. Wait, you want me to befriend who? But God, I've told everyone my plans. But now, I need to get a job and work where?"

The principles, precepts, and practices Julie and I share when we mentor others were given birth in the confusing and mundane experiences of the past. What I called wasted then were instead courses with lessons God knew we needed and that others would find helpful. Our transformation is always for the sake of others. Beyond that, God now uses people we helped to financially support so that we can share those so-called wasted experiences with you.

How crazy is that? Only God, with our cooperation, can make that happen.

What seemed wasted to me was developing my character and developing skills needed to leave my part of the planet better than I found it. I'm typically a cliché hater, so writing that last sentence surprised me.) Seriously though, you don't know what you don't know. Snap, I did it again—another cliché! What is happening to me? But really, God can be trusted with your future and since your future is uniquely yours, and nobody else's, your present circumstances probably look weird and wrong to you.

No words I write next can fix that confusion. Perhaps you are working a job you don't want. You work with a person or two who require extra grace. Your hairline is follicly challenged. Your best friend is dating your former boyfriend or you're living in an apartment with two other girls and only one bathroom. That is tough. No sugar can coat that medicine going down. As the kids' say, "I feel ya." The Good Father is working. Good plans are in your future. Hang on. Your adventure in faith awaits.

1. What part(s) of your story are you avoiding?
2. How might God be using this confusing season as an invitation to bring that part(s) of your story to Him and a trusted spiritual mentor for healing?
3. What experience(s) have you had that you can now see God was using for your good that you thought at the time were wasted?
4. Read and meditate on the experiences of the following biblical examples during their own "wasted" seasons: Moses in Midian (Exodus 2:15-3:1), Mary Magdalene at Jesus' tomb (John 20:1-15), and Rabbi Paul in Arabia (Galatians 1:11-18).

CHAPTER THREE

"Trapped by a Vision"

I WAS NOW CARRYING a burden for adults who were seeking a relationship with God in traditional weekend church services, but instead they found the content assumed insider knowledge they lacked and therefore, irrelevant as to why it mattered to them. Since I had experienced the power of the whisper I described in the previous chapter, it wasn't a surprise that I met an adult unchurched seeker. I was looking for opportunities to connect with people outside my Christian bubble. It wasn't surprising then, that I met a person open to following Jesus. The surprise was that I met him at church. You don't find unbelievers at church ... or so I mistakenly believed at the time.

I met him immediately after I'd given the benediction to dismiss the service. He was conspicuous there on the second row to my right, dressed in Texas western attire. We engaged in a brief conversation that led to me asking if he'd like to connect over breakfast or lunch. We settled on his day off that same week and sat down at a Furr's Cafeteria in East Dallas.

"So, Rick," I asked. "Tell me about you, how you found our church, and about your experience with your first visit?"

"I walked across the parking lot to get to your church," he began. "My parents live in a house nearby, and I've recently had to move back in with my youngest son. I'm going through a tough time."

"Tell me more," I pressed, the pastor in me inviting his pain. He went on to describe that he had recently ended his third marriage, had five children, was struggling with an addiction, and drowning in debt from alimony and child support payments. His milk route delivery wasn't enough, so he'd moved back in with his mom and dad to make ends meet.

"I'm 33 years old, Rod. My life isn't turning out like I'd hoped, obviously. As I was driving past your church last week on my way to work, a thought occurred to me, 'I wonder if there's anything in there for me?'"

I asked, "And was there... anything in there for you?" I could see Rick was hesitant to say, so I encouraged him. "Please, I want to hear from you about your experience."

"My son had a good experience. When I picked him up from the kids' space, he said he wanted to come back. I, on the other hand, felt out of place in my blue jeans and cowboy hat. You sang songs that were really old from a book that was hard to follow." (Note: Hymnals are weird in the way the stanzas are stacked.) Rick continued, "Your pastor told stories from a Book as if I knew them from a Book I don't even own. And I'm not wanting to be rude, Rod, but when you asked us to stand and grab hands with the person next to us to sing the closing song ... I'm a cowboy and I don't hold hands with no man, especially one I don't know." What Rick said next still rings in my ears as if it were yesterday: "It just seems to me that there ought to be a church for a guy like me to go to."

Selah. As I write that last sentence and reflect on that memory, I'm compelled to take my hands off the keyboard, sit back in my chair and stare out the window. I still feel Rick's heart-cry in my bones. Is there a church for a guy like Rick to go to? Who will give their attention to the unreached people groups in their own backyard without minimizing our mandate to take the message around the globe? Who will sacrifice their own preferences to use culturally sensitive language and methods like the apostle Paul did in Athens (Acts 17) to share the message of hope?

I thanked Rick for being candid and when I got home, I told Julie I knew something I wanted to give the rest of my life to... creating churches for the unchurched. Seekers deserve safe spaces. Rick met God and grew in his faith, despite the barriers that tradition and insider language presented. He met Diane at that same church and together they became a blended family. They remain committed to their faith and to each other to this day.

Confronted by this longing for environments to reach adults in less assumptive and nontraditional ways, we moved to central Missouri, taking bold steps in September 1988 to pursue this calling. The following May, I began a 30-day, juice-only fast seeking a divine vision to validate the meaningfulness of our decisions thus far and a motivation for what was to come. My disclaimer is that while I have a doctorate, I'm not a medical doctor. I now know more of the physical dangers I risked in doing so. I needed more medical oversight than I was aware of then. But that's what I did. Thirty days. Juice and water only.

I had multiple motivations for this extended fast. First, Jesus fasted before the start of his public ministry. I was on the cusp of starting mine. Second, I had read a book entitled, "Fast Your Way to Health" by J. Harold Smith. A third motivation was encouragement I'd once heard both Rick Warren and Don Sunukjian offer regarding our asking God for a vision. I heard them say that through prayer *and fasting,* you could ask God to give you a picture of something worth giving your life to and He might show you. And finally, I was so burdened that I didn't want to eat. I'm not sure I could have if I had tried. The plight of women and men open to the timeless truths of Jesus put off by culturally conditioned traditions and the assumptive language of His followers was heavy on me. And it still is.

The setting when the two-part vision I'm about to describe manifested was an early morning on Day 20 of this fast. I was driving from Excelsior Springs into Kansas City to attend the second day of a church conference when it happened. In my spiritual mind's eye, I saw a large room full of people and the facilitator asked the crowd this question: "How many of you changed the direction of your life as a result of a conversation you had with Rod?" Then many of the attendees stood. The meaning I make of this is that this is either my memorial service or a heavenly occasion.

Because of my familiarity with the concept of life-mapping from Robert Clinton's work "The Making of a Leader" (NavPress, 2nd ed., 2012), I now understand this ministry work is known as a divine appointment. A divine appointment occurs when a pivotal conversation presents a new way of thinking, or a choice becomes clear and a step of faith on the part of the recipient is required. I have exercised this spiritual gift multiple times throughout my ministry career, and some reading this may testify to having had this experience with me. To be clear, it is divine and sacred work. When it happens, I am a co-creator with God in the miraculous synergy of heaven meeting earth. It's not only me and it's not something that I can perform at will. Nor would I want to. Wisdom is more than propositional—it's personal. God is Wisdom.

Still driving toward Kansas City, I experienced a second picture. The first regarded a future occurrence, but this one spoke to the present. I found myself spiritually transported, not physically, to our public library on Broadway looking across the shallow valley and into the downtown area of Columbia, Missouri. To make the connection clear, the calling of the first part of the vision to sit with people navigating personal and corporate crises became location specific. Central Missouri seemed destined to become our permanent earthly home. In due time, this half of the vision would be a "burr in the backside" when things got tough. Vision shmision! Be careful what you pray for?

While still in Dallas, I had prayed that wherever we landed, we would be there for life. It sounded noble. It was a longing that still resonates with me. My parents modeled longevity in one ministry setting. Rick Warren said it was what he had prayed. I liked the idea. I had not counted what it would cost when things didn't work out and the money ran out. When it was hard for days, months and years ... in those moments the vision I'd hoped for felt more like a trap.

It's unnerving to write about this two-part vision I experienced in the spring of 1989, at the age of 28. I didn't share it with others for many years. It felt sacred, subjective, and sketchy if used inappropriately. I didn't want to be that guy who "heard from God" or "you should support our ministry because I've had a vision." When it has seemed appropriate to verbally share about it in various settings, I've done so.

Like the other miraculous gifts, I don't think my experience described above is universal for others, nor is it a sign of maturity. Instead, it was what I asked for in my immaturity and God gave it knowing I would need it. He has used it often to bolster my resilience when I have become so, so very, so overwhelmingly tempted to quit.

I haven't yet. **I'm trapped by a vision.**

YOUR STORY

Before the days of the Paw Patrol pups confronting Mayor Humdinger's shenanigans, we had Popeye the Sailor Man standing up to Bluto and his trouble-causing ways. Those my age can quote by memory what Popeye would say when he saw an injustice that boiled his blood. "That's all I can stands, an' I can't stands it no more!"

What is it that you can't stands no more? What injustice in your world needs confronting? What need captivates your attention enough to give a hoot about meeting? I'll bet my dollar on whatever that something is, it is connected to your younger self story.

I can't stand it when access to theological education through traditional higher education sources is too expensive for most these days. I can't stand it when rural and minority ministry leaders cannot afford hardcopy biblical commentaries and the latest scholarship on ministry hot topics. I'm grateful for podcasts, blogs, Zoom, and other digital resources that are helping to level a playing field of accessible resources for faith community leaders. Curating quality resources for under-resourced ministry leaders in our area is a passion of mine because of my story.

I was a kid who asked questions like these: What is circumcision anyway? Isn't that genocide? And, how can people choose if God knows it already? Except for Mom and Bob Choat, my volunteer youth leader, most people met my questions with something like this, "We believe in believing. You sure ask big questions!"

Can you see where I'm going with this? My commitment to resource ministry leaders through our theological study center goes well beyond the next gen leader getting helped. It is also about the younger me sitting in their church Sunday School room taking the Bible seriously. I want those ministry leaders to say, "That's a great question, Maya. I don't know the answer, but I know a place where we can find out. Let me get back to you on that."

I'm talking about me, but I'm intending to talk about you. What is it that you can't stand, can't stands it no more? What are your holy discontents? What is it when you see it done well that brings you joy? What activity or action helped you feel seen, soothed, safe, or secure in your story? These questions and more are fodder for your future self as you decide what to pursue vocationally or as a volunteer.

Did music or doodling or drama or photography resonate with your younger self? Then pursue kingdom impact through art. Did being outside and in nature help you connect with yourself, God, and others? Then pursue adventure through backpacking and Christian camping. Is social media a tool you want to use to influence for good instead of destruction? Do it. Do it poorly first if you must and learn to do it better as you go. As this cliché wisely says, "God rarely steers a parked car!"

1. Reflect on seven to ten positive key events or people in your past and put a word or two on a Post-It note to represent each one.
2. Do the same with seven to ten negative experiences.
3. Share these with a spiritual friend/mentor and ask God to show you "can't stands it no more" themes that emerge.[1]
4. Consider the example of Ruth as a Moabite who was resilient through loss and trusted Naomi and Naomi's God for her future, allowing her to become a key figure in Israel's history and a testament to God's redemptive work.

---

1   For more on this, I strongly commend to you Terry Walling's resources at Leader Breakthru. You can find a free video resource where he describes in greater detail what I have outlined here. LeaderBreakthru.com/timeline
    I did this work in the year 2000, during a morning workshop when we invited him here to mid-Missouri. This life-mapping work has been of great benefit in helping me navigate purpose and convergence.

CHAPTER FOUR

"You're going to hold a baby."

NFERTILITY IS SUCH A painful reality. From the early pages of Scripture, we hear the invitation of the Creator: "Be fruitful and multiply." Love shared between a couple usually carries with it an innate longing to share that love through reproduction. Julie and I wanted another baby to love, a sibling for the amazing little girl we already had. But like other couples who know the brutal reality of infertility, we weren't experiencing pregnancy.

I was driving home from the mall, traveling on Scott Boulevard, when I encountered the Whisperer's words, "Tell her (Julie), **'You're going to hold a baby!'"**

"I can't do that," I argued. "If it doesn't happen, it will only multiply her pain," I continued, not to mention my own disappointment that only in retrospect am I willing to admit.

It was a Sunday afternoon. The team responsible for tearing down what we'd set up that morning for our weekend service had concluded its work of wrapping cords, putting microphones back in their boxes, cleaning toys, etc. Everything was stored behind the curtains under the screens of the local theater we rented for weekly services. The following week, we'd do it all over again.

Julie had taken Miriam home and was busy preparing our lunch. The angst Julie and I shared that another month had gone by without a + sign on the pregnancy test was heavy as I was driving home. We were doing all we knew to do. Julie's research gave us confidence we were doing our part. The next step logically would be to see an infertility specialist, but our church-planting salary, along with my maintenance-man-at-McDonald's pay, combined with Julie's income from doing some childcare in our home, didn't include maternity insurance. Therefore, that next step was out of the question.

Like other husbands, I hated feeling inadequate. I wanted what my wife wanted. I wanted a baby too. I struggled knowing I was powerless to label us "expecting." The monthly lament we shared seemed exacerbated given the sacrifices Julie was making to pursue our unique calling. We had consensus, but I'd initiated a riskier vocational endeavor than most of our seminary peers. They signed up with the seminary's placement ministry. I didn't. They were interviewed by elder boards, offered salary packages with job descriptions. I celebrated their new ministry settings, but I couldn't do it with a clear conscience. Our call was *pioneering*, a different kind of ministry. In a college community where we only knew one family—my brother Rick, his wife, Linda, and their two boys—the challenges were many.

Julie was fully on board. She had experienced the circumstances that led to our situation and sought God also in affirmation of our faith adventure. That's who she is. Julie is who I've known her to be since we were teenagers in our church youth group. But that doesn't mean it wasn't incredibly hard for her. And it was hard on me seeing her in pain, wanting a good gift that I couldn't give her.

That's the backdrop for the unexpected encounter with the Holy Spirit that Sunday afternoon as I drove home. "Tell her she's going to hold a baby," was the whisper I heard.

Betting on God is risky business. Speaking for God is riskier still. Like the title of this book suggests, I didn't grow up charismatic. On top of that, I'm a five on the enneagram scale, which means I'm a researcher and lean heavily toward the rational. I'm so left-brained, I sometimes fall over. Both the college and seminary I attended were labeled cessationist. That means almost all the profs held that the more miraculous spiritual gifts ceased with the completion of the biblical canon. To put it plainly, cessationists hold to the belief that when the books of the Bible were written and affirmed as these and not these others, then speaking in tongues, visions, miraculous healings, and prophecy were no longer the way the Holy Spirit got divine work done.

It's true that while nearly all of the professors at Dallas Theological Seminary held to a cessationist view, there was at least one who didn't, and he had a contract with an exception. An asterisk in his signed agreement with the school meant he was unwilling to limit how God might want to get things done. My respect for Don Sunukjian was huge. It still is. We now know through neuroscience that people we experience as "happy to be with us" have a significantly better chance to influence us. Don was that kind of person for me. He was a professor with an impressive resume who was happy to be with a student like me while discussing a topic (pastoral ministry) about which we were both deeply passionate. As a result, I heeded Don's explicit, though subtle, admonitions to be a willing participant in unexpected and unexplainable Spirit workings.

I tell my daughters that if they read my private notebooks after I'm dead, they'll see that most of my journaling occurred when I was struggling the most. In times of stress, I am more dependent and teachable. Our spiritual antennas are often higher when stressed. Our choice to follow Jesus in our faith adventure should include our willingness to heed the invitation to hear directly from God.

I recall asking Julie to put down whatever was in her hands at the time. Standing in our nondescript kitchen on Hartford Road, I told her what I had experienced on my short drive home. "You're going to hold a baby," I said. I remember qualifying further with phrases like, "I don't know what it means exactly. I don't know if it's adoption, or kids in other countries, or something else entirely. But I know what I heard. It's a thought that wasn't my thought. I'm as sure as I can be. God wants you to know, you're going to hold a baby." And the following June, we did.

We named her Hannah Grace. Hannah means "grace." We've teased each other and her through the years that we needed grace and more grace to parent her. Since she was young, I've consistently said two things about Hannah. One is that she came out of the womb telling me how to do whatever it is I'm doing. Usually, I do it her way. And most of the time, I've come to learn that her way is the better way. Hannah has an innate sense of doing things more efficiently. Even when it didn't work out, I've been bolstered by her confidence and helped by her companionship in getting something done. Of course, in the moment, I've also felt irritated by being told what to do.

The other thing I've shared with others in describing Hannah is how she helped me see a world that I didn't even know existed. I don't have better words to describe what I mean by that, but I do have a memory with her to illustrate it.

I arrived home one brutally hot summer afternoon to find her in her swimsuit playing in the driveway with a super-duper super soaker in her two little hands. Hannah was squirting water from here to there like it was the water show at Branson Landing. When I was a kid, we played with water pistols, but they never measured longer than about six inches. The super soaker she was packing was as tall as she was, I'm sure. There I was, finely dressed in my dry clean-only suit, having just returned home from officiating a funeral. I didn't want it to get wet.

As soon as I stepped out of the driver's seat and closed the door, I said firmly, "Hannah, don't even think about it. I don't want to ..." She started at the top of my head and emptied her canister all the way to my toes. True to the name *super soaker*, I was soaked. In that moment, I'm sure my face was as hot as the sun. I was livid.

"Why did you do that?" I muttered angrily. And God as my witness, this is how that kindergartener answered, "It starts with an F and ends with an N. It's called FUN, Dad!" As if to say, "You should try it sometime, Dad. You might like it." My heart melted and the anger drained from my body. That wasn't the first time, and it wouldn't be the last time that my youngest daughter helped me get out of my head and in touch with my heart. Hannah has helped me to see the world in ways that start with an "F" and end with an "N." I've needed more FUN in my life and God taught it through a gift I couldn't ignore or refuse. Nor would I want to.

I'm mindful as I write this chapter of the way I started it: "Infertility is such a painful reality." Not getting from God what we are confident we need when we think we need it is so hard. The silence of heaven can be deafening. WAIT is a four-letter word. Waiting is torture. Some waiting goes unfulfilled. Brutal is an understatement to describe a miscarriage or the sudden death of an infant. The death of an adolescent or adult child is heartbreaking times ten. I've walked with many who are parenting a prodigal. The shame and blame we carry as parents is excruciating for anyone who is not living in denial.

I'm comforted to know that our God knows the lows and highs of parenting. In my theological framework, God doesn't get everything God ultimately wants. His ideal will *is not* always done. However, His redemptive will *is*. I hold that while our Heavenly Father has exhaustive foreknowledge of all things His children will suffer, they are not necessarily His will. Known by God but not determined by God. This view is known as paradoxical indeterminism. Nature and human agency are in play. Therefore God, as the ultimate Good Parent, empathizes with us as parents experiencing children with their own agency and willing rebellion rather than flourishing. God grieves with us in loss. God waits with us as creation groans (Romans 8:22) under the weight of sin's curse. Together with God we await a coming day when all things are made new. God is holding our tears until that day. In the now, but not quite yet, the Holy Spirit draws seekers, intercedes for believers and sometimes whispers divine instructions to help us keep the faith.

YOUR STORY

If you're reading this and being reminded of your own heartache, I'm wondering how you are letting others be with you in your pain. Or perhaps it is more accurately said—**not** letting others walk with you in the disappointment that is cutting so deep. The way a friend or spouse fails to validate your grief only exacerbates your hurting. Isolation seems better than risking relational connection and being further disappointed. Let me oversimplify some tools that may help you navigate this complex dance between suffering alone and companioning together:

Introverts/Extroverts[1]
- Introverts like to think before they speak. Extroverts need to speak to think.
- Introverts need solitude to replenish. Extroverts replenish through relating.
- Introverts tend to manage momentum. Extroverts tend to create momentum.

Volunteers/Invite-onlys[2]
- Volunteers share without having to be asked. Invite-onlys only share when asked.
- Volunteers think asking questions is prying. Invite-onlys think sharing unless asked is imposing.
- Volunteers assume others will share when ready. Invite-onlys assume if others care, they'll ask.

1 Here's a resource I found helpful on this topic: *Introverts in the Church: Finding Our Place in an Extroverted Culture*. Adam S. McHugh. IVP, 2009. 222p.
2 For more on the invite-only type: HaileyMagee.com/blog/category/Communication

As an introvert with an invite-only personality bent, I now realize I can be quite confusing to my spouse, children, and peers. As an introvert, I appear physically calm, cool, and collected. But internally, I'm anxiously processing tons of information at once and often emotionally flooded. It was a breakthrough day when I learned I needed to be verbally reminded, "Use your words, Rod. We can't hear what you're thinking!"

As an invite-only type, I carry my apprehensions close to the vest. I think peers don't care. They think I'm fine. On my worst days, I'm asking them how they're doing, while wishing the whole time they'd ask me how I'm doing.

On the flip side, I can imagine you as an extrovert volunteering your heartaches and finding blank stares looking back at you. Perhaps, you think you are too much, and people can't handle your sharing. You can't not share but when you do, you wish you hadn't. That's hard too.

I'm hesitant to say what I'm about to for fear of spiritualizing away your present struggle. It's not my intention to minimize. As apprentices of Jesus, He is our go-to. He listens. He cares. His Spirit comforts. He prays to the Father on our behalf. As Julie reminds me, Jesus is the milkshake, and people are the whipped cream and cherry on top. If you can get whipped cream and a cherry on top, that's an added benefit. But when we can't, we're not at a deficit. Jesus is our entrée.

People can be Jesus with skin on, and that's cool too. The body of Christ is a physical manifestation of His grace. On our better days, we show up for each other in ways that mirror His tender correction and His firm support. Don't grow weary in learning how to communicate with each other. Don't shut down and live isolated. Ask God for resources needed to grow in your awareness of how you are wired, and how that's different from your spouse or closest spiritual friends.

1. What personality type listed above do you most closely identify with?
2. Reflect on a time when you were hurting and someone showed up for you in a life-giving way.
3. How could you plan a spiritual retreat for a time of solitude and prayerful contemplation?
4. In Acts 15:36-41 we read of a sharp disagreement between two ministry partners. What lessons can we learn from their example?

CHAPTER FIVE

"Just WAIT, I'm working."

———

A LL THE SIGNS were pointing to the reality that our church start, Spring Valley Community Church (SVCC), was ending. The five years of its life had provided space for Julie and me to grow up, learn faithfulness, and practice pastoring. The 30 or so who identified SVCC as their faith community were loyal, perhaps to a fault, and among the kindest people we have ever known. There was no Plan B. Together we felt stuck. We couldn't keep going. Something had to change.

Five years earlier, our official launch hadn't yielded the critical mass we had hoped for. The attendance numbered 44. The largest attendance we had for the five years we were together was our inaugural Sunday in October 1989. Those years were filled with transformation—no doubt about that—but it wasn't sustainable. That reality became abundantly clear in the summer of 1994.

We had moved out of the Columbia Mall Theaters and rented space from the Immanuel Christian Reformed Church on Sunday evenings. That decision provided financial relief but yielded little in the way of momentum for the church's future. Perhaps if I had known then about the micro church movement and a missional template we might have stayed together. But given what we did know, we were at the end of a road with no outlet.

I'd been able to go from full-time to very part-time employment at the Stadium McDonald's due to the generosity of the Iowa District of the Baptist General Conference (now Convergence). However, the denomination's $1,000 monthly investment was coming to an end, having fulfilled its three-year commitment. That gift had been especially generous given the fact that I had failed their church planting assessment. Their leadership had wisely determined that my giftings did not fit the criteria of a pioneering planter, nor that of a senior pastor. I didn't disagree. In fact, I affirmed it. But what was I to do? I felt trapped by a vision. I didn't want to wear the golden arches uniform anymore. I wanted traditional church employment.

Like you, I am frequently asked by other of Jesus' followers, "What is your home church?" My heartfelt answer to that question is this: "The one we started when we first got here." Regardless of where else I've been a member, nothing compares to the ecclesia (church life) I experienced there. Spring Valley Church was my baby, and I still grieve the loss of her.

But that summer it was obvious it was over. We couldn't find an affordable space to meet. My giftings weren't a match for what that church needed. Our best discernment efforts couldn't see a future. It had been a good run and it was now time to let it die.

I resolved to do what I had been unwilling—unable really—to do previously. I resolved to contact the placement office of my alma mater and submit my resume as a candidate for a support role on a ministry staff somewhere that wanted "a Dallas man," a common reference in that world to describe the theological tribe looking for a Dallas Theological Seminary graduate.

Given my philosophical restlessness with some of the straitjacket assumptions that come with that association, it was a hard pill to swallow. Also, I would be forced to abandon the location-specific spiritual vision I had encountered during my extended spiritual fast. My processing went like this. It was God's vision, not mine. In effect, I surrendered even the right to have a vision at all and I think that was an essential variable in that season's growth.

No sooner had I opened my hands, finally willing to explore leaving central Missouri, than the power of a whisper once again became a disrupter. I went to sleep in my bed, but I awoke promptly at 2 a.m. I settled into a family room chair and experienced a thought that wasn't my thought. It became the same thought three mornings in a row. It was a thought so strong that I couldn't shake it. I had no idea what it meant in real life, and no way of knowing how it would play out in tangible ways for us. It was a thought that left me feeling helpless and vulnerable, yet somehow strangely hopeful. At least now I'd had enough experience with these kinds of thoughts that I recognized it as divinely initiated. And the thought was this: **"Just WAIT. I'm working."**

Working on what? No answer. My consolation was a book by Ben Patterson entitled, "Waiting: Finding Hope When God Seems Silent." (IVP, 1990, 170 p.)

A backdrop to this w-a-i-t-i-n-g season was fulfilling a commitment I had made to a ministry colleague. The founding pastor of Columbia's Woodcrest Chapel (WC), a bustling faith community in the southwest corner of our small city, had called me months before to tell me he was "burned out, resigning, divorcing, and moving." As a ministry peer, he asked me to do three things for him: 1. Visit the hospital to minister to a single woman with a terminal illness; 2. Finish a premarital counseling commitment and officiate a couple's wedding; 3. Check in on the three remaining staff members of the church he was leaving. In due time, it was revealed he wasn't merely leaving. He was abandoning his commitments and calling. His behavior had been scandalous, and he was getting out of Dodge before it all came to light. Regardless, completing these three commitments put me in contact with that faith community.

Since our band of believers was meeting on Sunday evenings, I was available on Sunday mornings to "fill the pulpit" as we call it in church-speak. The leadership of WC invited me to preach for them a time or two while they were looking for a candidate to be their senior pastor. I had been taught by my mentors that the world's system was the competition, not other churches. When one of us was hurting, we all hurt. And vice versa. When one of us had a win, we all won. Given all this exposure, you might think that I began to wonder about my own participation in Woodcrest Chapel's future. But I didn't. The question of whether we might merge didn't happen until months later.

When Pieter, the newly called senior pastor of Woodcrest, asked the event planning team to include me in the program for his ordination and a welcome reception in late summer, only then did it occur to me that I might want to participate in the next chapter of this church's life. I brought a "welcome to the area as a representative from other area ministers" message at the event. It wasn't until then that I wondered if God was knitting our hearts to theirs. The thought was bittersweet. I didn't want Spring Valley Community Church to die. We couldn't sustain what we were doing, however.

I wondered if Woodcrest Chapel might be (that is, continue to be) the kind of "safe space for seekers and disciple them to full maturity" that I was committed to being a part of.

After Pieter moved to Columbia and began his new duties, I felt prompted to introduce him to other pastors around town, entertain his family in our home, and invite him to come share a message with our Spring Valley folks at one of our Sunday evening gatherings. He did, and these invitations gave us space to hear each other's history, tell our ministry experiences, share theological priorities, and discuss missional strategy. There was much that aligned us. The things we thought about differently were things we could hold loosely.

During the remaining fall months, our conversation turned to the possibility of my employment and merging our small congregation with theirs. I'd assessed by this time I didn't want to be responsible for the weekly teaching a senior pastor role demanded. My introverted personality felt confident that an associate staff role would fit me better. I wanted to lead from a chair different from the one sitting at the head of the table (the lead pastor under Jesus, of course).

The "Just w.a.i.t., I'm working" whisper I'd heard in July was severely tested during the following four months. Why does Spring Valley have to end? What if we received an unexpected financial gift to keep her going? Are we giving up too soon? Woodcrest was reeling from the founding pastor's sudden exit. How hard will it be to transition to new leadership? How are we going to make it financially if we stay in Columbia? Will our two daughters adjust to a new community? How will the WC staff welcome a new kid on their block, especially one from across town whose recent resume includes being a McDonald's employee and failed church planter? These questions and more were the fabric of this waiting period.

Writing it now doesn't seem that big of a deal, but when you're the one waiting on God for an answer, it feels like forever. Can I get a witness?

I got an unexpected phone call from Piet just before Thanksgiving offering me a position with the title, "Director of Singles and Outreach." The title "Pastor" wasn't a part of the description, which was even more challenging for me to come to terms with than the $24,000 salary offer with no health insurance. We were used to financial sacrifice but relinquishing the identity I found in my educational and vocational pursuits was tough.

Regardless, we had confidence that God had been working. Despite the grief of Spring Valley Church's era ending, we felt assured of God's redemptive plan in this new endeavor. Many of our small group made the transition with us and I began my new assignment on January 2, 1995.

Writing this chapter describing the transition from a church planter to an associate pastor hasn't been easy. The end of our time at Woodcrest Chapel included scandal, trauma, unresolved conflict, heartbreak, NDAs, and scriptural violations on the part of a board of directors and a few staff members. That part of our story is included in the "Afterword."

Despite this ending, my hard-fought healing now includes an axiom that the end of things is not the sum of it. The way something concludes does not negate its value. That thinking is too transactional, and wisdom literature such as the book of Job refutes it. Following Jesus includes Garden of Gethsemane-like suffering. The too-familiar institutional systemic evil that ended our two decades of serving Woodcrest Chapel doesn't invalidate the experiences that got us there. Nor should the many God-moments we shared while there be diminished.

Whether God led us or let us, He used it for good.

YOUR STORY

Imagine yourself sitting in a boardroom. Picture Jesus in the CEO seat and you are to his immediate right. This is your personal board of directors. The agenda is your life; the purpose is to consider your past, to make sense of your present and thereby enable your future to flourish. Who else is seated around the table? What voices are you getting counsel from? Are some of the chairs empty? Are there people there that you want to replace with other people? Let me unpack what I'm doing with what I am saying.

Julie quotes Pete Scazzero, the emotionally healthy spirituality authority, often saying, "We have Jesus in our hearts, but Grandpa in our bones!" And "Every church board member has nine people, figuratively speaking, sitting at the table behind them." Who are the nine people behind you?

What coach told you you're not disciplined enough to handle what life is going to throw at you? What older cousin said you were only acceptable when you were cracking jokes? What boss called you below average? What boss said you were above average and ought to be more productive? Did a parent communicate you were destined for greatness, and you're left exhausted trying to high jump an invisible bar? Where did you come to misbelieve that you had to perform to be loved? Where did you hear that if you don't have at least $500k in your retirement portfolio you're a failure? What teacher told you, "You can be anything you want to be," only for you to find out you can't. What preacher taught you God's will is like the bullseye of a target and you're convinced you missed it? These are the voices in our heads sitting around the conference table who make up our personal board of directors.

You can't deny they are there, but you can argue with them. You can unseat them. You can tell them to stop talking. But most importantly, you can invite new people to join Jesus in your executive boardroom. May I suggest a few roles to consider adding if no one is filling that seat already?

- A fun friend(s)—someone you share a hobby with, probably someone you don't work with, someone who doesn't care that you're a big deal in your world. Friends care more about you than they do about your ministry. They congratulate you on the article you published and when you ask them if they want to read it, they feel free to say no.
- A prayer warrior—someone you tell what's really going on, who regularly takes you to the throne room of God and intercedes on your behalf.
- An older mentor—someone who picks up your calls and answers your texts. If they have been known to text you unprompted, you've struck gold. These aged sages are question-askers and are willing to tell you their stories and then

will tell you the rest of the story. The rest won't be easy for them to tell; you'll have to dig for it. But if they share it, there's pure wisdom for you to heed. A mentor cares about you and more than you—they care about the mission of your ministry too.

- A professional counselor—someone trained with therapeutic skills. I think of them like a farmer plowing the soil of my soul, asking good questions, bringing weeds and rocks to the surface and helping sow healthier seeds.

- Ministry partner(s)—peers who ask, "How can we be with you today?" Partners care more about the mission than they care about you.

- And more: a spiritual director, a financial consultant, a professional coach, and _____. These are roles I've not taken advantage of, at least not yet, but I see the wisdom of adding them.

A reason what I've written here matters to me as much as it does is because I didn't value this in my early ministry years the way I now wish I had. Some of the reasons for not doing so were circumstantial. Others related to my personality type. I didn't see it modeled. I don't recall it being taught or written about in the literature I was reading or the classrooms preparing me for pastoral ministry. Regardless, in the encounter shared in this chapter and the earlier ones, I was mostly unaware of who I was allowing to sit on the governing board of my decision-making. I was late in my 30s before I began the work of intentionally quieting louder voices and inviting others, etc. It's a deeply unfortunate revelation to declare that my prior intel was lacking. Learn from my lack. With Jesus at the head of your table, recruit and receive life-giving resources from an intentional group to help you stay the course and finish strong.

1. What voice(s) in your head do you need to quiet or replace?
2. What misbeliefs are they shouting that need to be processed with a mentor, spiritual director, coach, pastor, or peer?
3. Spend some time with the biblical perspective of God in trinitarian form consulting with a divine council in Job 1:6-12, 2:1-7; Psalm 82; and I Kings 22:19-23. What do you make of this and how might it inform your value of others in navigating your own life?
4. Write some emails/texts/notes this week to thank those who participate in making a positive contribution to your personal board of directors.

CHAPTER SIX

"A deceiving spirit? That's on YOU!"

———

"I **NEED TO TELL YOU** something," I said to Julie as she came into the living room one morning. She put her coffee on the coaster nearby and looked in my direction.

"I've been online during the night looking at ..." her eyes widened as if I was about to confess something. "No, no, not that!" I hurriedly reported. "I'm looking at teaching positions available. I think it's time we move. It's time I become a seminary professor. And guess what? There's an opening in Dallas, our alma mater!" I said excitedly.

Her gaze did not match my enthusiasm. "I don't think God is in it," she said candidly.

"But, babe, you love the Dallas area. You could work with seminary spouses, lead emotionally healthy small groups like you do here, and make an investment in them just like Chaplain Bryan's wife, Shirley, did for you!" I pleaded.

"I don't see it," was all I could get from her. Her skepticism was well grounded. Read on and you'll discover why.

57

Just a few weeks prior, we'd received news that rocked our ministry world. My boss, our lead pastor, announced in our Pastoral Advisory Team lunch meeting that he had three to five years left in him to serve and then he was leaving. While my title was senior associate pastor, my working role was chief consultant. My practical calling was to help the lead pastor and staff make better decisions, both personally and corporately. In short, if he wasn't leading, I didn't have a role. I had a job, but the reason for joining the Woodcrest Chapel (WC) team 19 years earlier was ending. I wrote out a resignation letter that I never submitted, which illustrates the frame of mind I was in.

There are a couple of things you should know before I get to the unexpected whisper I experienced just a few months later. First, it was no secret that I wanted to teach in a bible college or seminary. Years earlier when I was asked about my future, I'd told the church leadership who oversaw my hiring, "When my daughters are in high school or so, I'm going to go teach somewhere. I want to make an investment in the next generation of ministry leaders like the one invested in me!" I even considered a Ph.D. program in communication but instead pursued BIOLA/Talbot Seminary's Doctor of Ministry degree. That terminal degree limited me to the Pastoral Ministries department in theological education. That fit me just fine; that was where I wanted to teach anyway.

Second, two years earlier, we had incorporated the Theological Education Initiative (TEI) as a nonprofit entity. While it was physically and financially embedded within Woodcrest Chapel, it was legally separated from it. Our lectures, library, institute, and scholarships were an outreach arm for area ministry leaders while I was still employed as a WC pastor.

Over the course of the next couple of months, I brought up the subject to Julie, always encouraging her to consider the great adventure we'd have together in a teaching profession. Each time she patiently listened, while I felt discouraged that her excitement wasn't matching mine. In mid-October, we flew to southern California, settled into our hotel, and I drove to BIOLA University for the 2014 gathering of the Evangelical Homiletics (EHS). The EHS is a professional organization where teachers of preaching, and some pastors who are passionate about the subject, meet for a few days at a host school for fellowship and where they can further develop their homiletical/preaching craft. Pedagogy and best practices are the primary focus for attending, but this year my overwhelming motivation was to get offered a job.

Sure enough, all the people with whom I had hoped to network were there—Timothy Warren and Vic Anderson in particular, both former teaching assistants while I was a student. Now they were tenured professors and hiring a new colleague. If only I could make them aware of my adjunct teaching experience and my readiness for a vocational transition, we could get the employment ball rolling. The subject didn't come up during our social meet-and-greet in the courtyard, but we still had a couple of days together where it could happen.

After dinner and hearing from plenary speaker Jack Hayford that evening, I hung around until I was alone with Don Sunukjian. He had been out to Columbia, Missouri, a few times to teach preaching and preach to our Woodcrest community. Our conversation went just as I'd hoped.

"How's it going in central Missouri?" he asked.

"Not good," I answered.

"Oh yeah? What's up?"

"Our senior pastor has announced he's all but done. I'm confident he doesn't want to be there any longer and if he's not leading and creating, my calling there is through," I said.

"What are you going to do, Rod?" Don was saying the very words I envisioned hearing.

"I want to teach in a pastoral ministries department. I want to do for the next generation what you did for me so many years ago and what you're still doing," I said. "The reviews from my part-time teaching gigs at A.W. Tozer and Bethel Seminaries are quite positive," I continued. "And I love doing it!" I added jubilantly.

"I could totally see you doing that," Don told me. "When you get ready to make that move, let me know and I'll help you."

Instead of feeling encouraged, my spirit ran cold and I didn't know what that meant in the moment. He said the very words I longed to hear from him regarding an affirmation of my transition from pastor to professor, and I felt a cold chill. I excused myself and went back to the hotel with a disoriented soul. That would prove to be the first of three uneasy encounters I'd have while attending EHS.

Late the next morning, Pastor Hayford, then 80 years of age, shared with the attendees an experience he'd had as a younger minister. He had found himself obsessed with lust for another woman employed in the offices of the Foursquare denominational offices. He added that he'd never acted out on his infatuation and described how he prayed for victory from this constant ministry distraction.

I was rolling my eyes as this Pentecostal, Promise Keeper octogenarian confessed his sexual temptation from so long ago. Until I heard him say, "I could tell you exactly where I was in the denominational hallway when it left me. It was a deceiving spirit."

"A deceiving spirit? How ridiculous!" I thought so loud I might have wondered if those around me heard it. Here's a charismatic pastor in an academic setting telling a story about his struggle with lust and blaming a demonic force. That's what my brain was processing when I encountered another thought, not my own. That Thought whispered, **"A deceiving spirit? That's on you!"**

In seconds, my posture pivoted 180 degrees. My dismissive judging turned to rapt attention. "There are two ways you know if you have a deceiving spirit," the man who was now a sage to me continued. "First, it is always self-serving."

I wrote it in my notebook lying next to my open Bible. Guilty on count one, I reasoned, knowing in my gut that a tsunami was brewing in the faith community I served. My motivation for leaving central Missouri wasn't altogether altruistic. It was self-preserving. I didn't want to be around when the hooey hit the fan; and unbeknownst to me, the first strong wind blew less than a year later.

I was ready to write down the second way you know when it's a deceiving spirit, but perhaps because of his age he forgot to tell it. It didn't matter. The Spirit told me what He wanted me to know, and I wrote … play it out over the next eight or nine years. Soon afterward I found myself transported into the classroom, imagining for myself a life of grading papers, enduring department meetings, and telling the same old stories about the days when I used to be on the front lines of church life. In addition to that, I was a stranger in a new city, missing my Panera Bread iced tea and sick in a hospital where I was just another patient instead of a respected minister in the community. A deceiving spirit. That was on me. Could it be? That was two unexpected encounters. The third happened later that same day.

The only thing I knew about Cal Pearson was that he had taught homiletics for many years at Southwestern Baptist Theological Seminary. When I arrived for dinner that evening, I found myself seated next to him in the dining room. I reminded him of my name and that he had been a year ahead of me in the Pastoral Ministries department at Dallas. "So, how's it going there in Fort Worth?" I asked, thinking I was making casual conversation.

I was taken aback when he replied, "I'm not in Fort Worth anymore. I'm pastoring in Houston these days."

"No kidding! Tell me about it." Mind you, Cal had zero knowledge I was trying to transition from pastoring to teaching. He hesitated by saying it was a long story, but when I insisted, he summarized his experiences this way, "I grew discontent with several things in higher education. First, you must vet every decision. It can be frustrating for a leader, and you look to me like a leader, Rod. You'd hate it."

"Also, my ministry stories got old in the classroom with each passing year. I was telling the students examples of God at work from decades ago. I longed to tell new stories," he said. "And lastly, I tired of grieving the relationships lost with students graduating and moving on to their ministry assignments. They promised to keep in touch but rarely did. I missed them."

Cal had no way of knowing the ministry leaders I was mentoring back in Missouri had relational longevity. There are too many to name, but I'll offer John Drage as an example. Drage and I met together for many years over coffee to discuss personal and ministry challenges. We had already begun incorporating our Theological Education Initiative with its resources for area emerging church and campus leaders. Cal did not know that I had been seriously trying to leave all this for a teaching position when he concluded with one last thought. "I'll tell you this, Rod. Pastoring is ten times harder than teaching. So, if you're looking for an easier gig, you ought to take it!"

Internally, I threw up both hands in surrender and whispered back toward heaven, "I hear You, Lord. I give. I'll stay in central Missouri."

It became clear to me what I really wanted was an easier assignment than the one I was experiencing. I wanted out of the institutional dysfunction that was swirling at the center of the church I had a role in. The primary reason I said yes to serving there ended when the senior pastor announced he was quitting. I didn't want the trouble that I knew in my gut was heading in our direction. I also wanted to spend more time mentoring the next generation of ministry leaders. Relief was coming in due time, but not without pain first.

Later that night, while holding Julie's hand and walking in Downtown Disney, I told her about the three unexpected encounters of the past 24 hours.

"I told you God wasn't in it," she said with a wink.

YOUR STORY

As ministry leaders, we like to play mind *games* when we're discouraged. One is the *greener grass* game. In this game, we tell ourselves that others have it better than we do. Large churches have an advantage because they have more staff and a bigger budget. Or smaller churches don't have to worry about safety issues in the nursery or recruiting enough volunteers to hold doors and greet newcomers at multiple entrances.

Support (parachurch) ministry leaders tire of raising all their financial support and long for a stable employer—"If only I could work where I didn't have to raise all my own support." Campus staff endure a 25 percent turnover rate every school year. They're not done grieving the loss of their graduated senior leadership while needing to recruit incoming freshmen during welcome week each fall. If only they could find a job that paid well, then they could serve on campus as a volunteer and give financially to support it. And the beat goes on.

The greener grass game was a variable in my encounter you just read about in this chapter. That's not to invalidate the necessary endings. Goodbyes are part and parcel of reality. "For a reason, for a season" is a motto that helps me grieve lost relationships and welcome new ones. But now looking in the rearview mirror I didn't want to leave pastoring in central Missouri; I just didn't see a way clear to the other side of the impending struggle. God, in His mercy, got my attention and stopped me from climbing the fence only to find *different* grass, not *better* grass on the other side.

Another game I find myself playing when I'm discouraged is the *I would have been great at [fill in the blank]*. I would have been a great lawyer. I would have been great if only I'd become a financial advisor. I would have been great if only I'd listened to my friend when she invited me to join her in that "Shark Tank" entrepreneurial endeavor. And we always add, "And I would have made a lot more money."

For the third mind game, let's call it the *game of rabble*. In the biblical account of the Exodus from Egypt, we read about the response of Moses when some of the people, the Bible calls them "the rabble," begin griping about the manna God provided and declaring they were better off in Egypt as slaves. How did Moses respond? By playing the *game of rabble*. Projecting on Moses's candor in Numbers 11:10-15, below is my paraphrase on what it sounds like when we play the game of rabble and blame all the ministry failures on others.

"God, these people you gave me are impossible. I don't deserve this. If only I had different people to work with, we could get something done around here. How am I supposed to fulfill the

vision you gave me with them? What have I done to deserve this trouble? Go ahead, slay me. I can't do it. I quit."

These three games we play (greener grass, I would have been great at _____, and the game of rabble) are distractions from the Christ-like character qualities God is forming in us through these experiences. What we may need, rather than resign, is to calm our overwhelmed nervous system, get to the root of what we are feeling and why we are feeling it, re-engage our executive reasoning, and turn our attention to hear from God. Dreaming, projecting, and blaming are human, but futile. It's time we faced the truth.

The cold hard truth is we're probably doing the only thing we can do. We're probably making the kind of money we need to keep our feet on the ground. We would likely hate doing the greener grass job anyway. We very well might have made a mess of whatever we think we could or should have done.

More truth is that every vocation has its benefits and hardships. I think of first responders with the promise of a pension at the end of 20-year commitment but put their very lives on the line every time they respond to a call. School teachers enjoy a break in the summer but take calls from angry parents at night. Ministry leaders have flexible schedules but every six days a spiritually enriching worship event needs planning. Funerals, hospital visits, staff conflict, board nominations, and scandals need attention in between.

Maybe you do need to make a major vocational change, but for me (and I suspect for many of you), I'm convinced we're doing what God has gifted us to do. What we need is not a wholesale change, but significant shifts within the ministry paradigm we find ourselves in.

If sermon preparation drains you, perhaps building a teaching team around you is needed. If your therapy practice insurance and paperwork have become a nightmare, consider a less formal professional coaching template instead. Maybe high school students aren't your vibe after all, so prayerfully consider a role in the social sector. What certification or degree will enhance your options? For me, my transition was from local church work to a seminary-like study center. I still pastor, but specifically, I pastor pastors and our ministry supporters. Sincere empathy and prayers for you as navigate these transitions for yourself.

1. Name where you feel trapped in your current situation. What emotions are you having and why? I feel _____ because _____ _____.

2. Who can be with you, without trying to fix it, as you navigate some needed modifications to your responsibilities and schedule?

3. Continue asking God for resources to give you clarity and resilience to endure until you do.

4. Consider the biblical account of Moses and the rabble (Numbers 11:4-6;10-15). How are you comforted and challenged by the discouragement this hero of the faith verbalized? Do you give yourself permission to be as candid with God as Moses was about the difficult people in your ministry?

My parents — Rev. Gene & Joyce Casey

Mom reading a poem for
the church radio program

The Casey Family, from left — Randy, Joyce, Rick, Gene, Rod, Jan & Ron

My Shetland pony, Taffy, and her colt

Like many kids, I hoped to play in the Pros one day.

Our Wedding Day — June 2, 1984
Hopes. Dreams. A Faith Adventure.

Julie & I graduating from Tennessee Temple University, 1982

Our daughters —
Miriam (15) & Hannah (10)

Our grandchildren —
Silas, Oliver, Lydia & Lucy

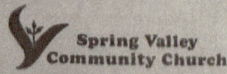

An ad for our church plant, 1992

A passion of mine — persuasive preaching

It was a "big deal" to have a headline in the local paper, 1989

Woodcrest Chapel

My ministry peers for two decades

A silhouette of me showing
the heavy burdens ministry can bring

Teaching theology in our Church Leadership Institute

Entrance to our Christian Resource Center, located in the Parkade Center

CHAPTER SEVEN

"8,500"

"**P**LEASE, DON'T DO THIS**,**" I pleaded. "You will be creating a second offense for me by violating the Scripture to 'Not take your brother to court.' (I Corinthians 6:1-7) You can't mean this unless you intend to sue us if we break it." My voice broke with each word I spoke. The manilla envelope containing the severance check and the non-disclosure agreement (NDA) was still in the hand of the church's board president.

The first offense to which I am referring was the reinstatement of the senior pastor in early June. When the news broke that the board of directors, along with the staff management team, considered restoring him so soon after the discipline of his pastoral ethics violations, Julie and I made our intentions clear. If he was prematurely reinstated, we would resign. My first appeal was to the senior pastor. "Don't do this," I said. "You're not ready. You don't meet two of the biblical qualifications for serving as the ruling elder. You're not yet proven to be 'above reproach,' nor do you have a 'good reputation among outsiders.' And know this," I continued. "If you do—the day before you are reinstated will be my last day identifying as a pastor here."

Over the weeks following, we repeated this admonition to the staff and then to the entire board of directors.

The admonition went unheeded, and, true to my word, I resigned on June 4. Since I was the one who resigned, it's accurate to say

that my employer owed me nothing other than the standard severance of unpaid days, COBRA, etc. It is also accurate to suggest
their offer to provide a paycheck through the summer could be
considered generous, though I had hoped for six months instead.
But given the fact that Julie and I had served sacrificially for 21
years and that the premature reinstatement came in a matter of
weeks instead of months, it is also true that three months wasn't
enough given the circumstances. Financially speaking, it was
about as bad as it could get. Or so we thought.

The conversation with the board president was about to make
things a lot worse. "This check includes you signing something
you're not going to like," she said. "It's a legal document that
includes the commitment *neither you nor your spouse will
discuss the circumstances leading up to, nor the reasons for, your
resignation.*" Holding back emotion, I expressed how offended I
was by it and that it had never been done during my time on staff,
nor would I have ever allowed it. I begged her to take it back and
not insist that I take it.

Our time ended with her agreement to reconsider and get the
matter settled differently. It didn't. The document, bank check,
and a letter informing us the check was null and void until the
document was returned signed, was sent to our home via certified
mail in early August. We refused to sign it. We held it in our hands
while we prayed for strength to forgive and God to provide, then
put it in our ministry scrapbook with other reminders of our faith
adventures.[1]

---

1   Whatever the motivations, months later we received another bank check in the mail with a letter saying,
"Please accept this check with no strings attached in recognition of your years of ministry among us." I
would have appreciated an apology to accompany it as well.

It never occurred to me that a Christian ministry would require an NDA from one of its staff members. It's worth noting these events took place before the now infamous #metoo and #churchtoo scandals. I had never heard of a church participating in such a worldly, judicial, truth-suppressing, corporate method. The very thought of threatening legal action within a faith community still knots my stomach. I'm not suggesting there are no religious situations to ensure accountability that might warrant criminal and civil action, but this situation was about suppressing truth in the hope of saving institutional face. Frankly, I'm embarrassed that a group of people I helped disciple would participate in such an institutional evil. On the other end of the continuum, I'm so grateful Julie wholeheartedly agreed that we shouldn't sign it and valued telling the truth over our financial security.

As people in ministry, I had long insisted we get our paycheck from Jesus, not merely from an organization. This hypothesis was being tested. No matter the rationale of the church leadership, our refusal to sign the NDA and thereby participate in the attempted cover-up, meant we were going through our limited savings account fast. I find God is rarely early, but never late. Providentially, there was a solution surfacing that might be able to help.

I knew of Reliant Mission because of our long association with John Drage and The Rock Church on the campus of the University of Missouri. I came to find out in a hurry that Reliant partners with other nonprofit gospel-centered organizations providing effective fundraising tools (training and coaching) and back-office support (payroll and benefits). Our Theological Education Initiative (TEI) fit the criteria, and not only did John vouch for us, but he also graciously introduced us to some key people to help. Soon after, we registered for an eight-day staff orientation which offered intensive coaching on how to raise missionary support. Julie and I flew to Orlando in late August to become the full-time missionaries we are today.

While a newbie to the world of mission agencies, I had lived my entire life familiar with the tradition of supporting pastoral staff through freewill offerings, including contributions from the church to support some missionaries. This thinking mirrored our personal budget. To consider asking family, friends, and nearly anybody to hear our presentation and give financially beyond whatever they gave to their own spiritual community was unfamiliar and unquestionably daunting. But something far more daunting than raising support was the threat of not continuing our work of mentoring next generation leaders through the TEI. To do so, the back-office administrative support including group health insurance, self-employment taxes, workers compensation, IRS-compliant policies and procedures, etc. were needed, and Reliant was that provider.

Beyond the paperwork, policy and procedures instruction, most of our time in Orlando was spent preparing and practicing our fundraising presentations. In retrospect, it seems like it should have been easier than it was to coalesce our heart for under-resourced ministry leaders and find some pictures to go with it. But it wasn't easy; it was demanding.

At the same time, we compiled a list of names of people we knew, had once known, wish we knew—anyone we could ask to meet with us to share our pitch and invite them to join our support team. I was no stranger to this strategy. Indeed, I had experience with it as a pastor. The introvert in me shriveled at the prospect. I "ugly cried" three times during our eight days in Orlando. Julie and I were the oldest missionary recruits in the room by a long shot. I struggled with feeling shame. There must be something terribly wrong with me, I was implicitly feeling, to have this kind of dramatic transition at this point in my vocational career. I was reminded how God sometimes asks us to do hard things. He invites us to stretch our faith in ways beyond our present capacity. God does give more than *we* can handle. This was going to be one of those times.

Part of our orientation included the setting of a support goal. As we added ours, the number felt astronomical. Not because it was. Our paycheck was modest and well within what's called "industry standards." The reason it felt overwhelming was because we were responsible for 100% of the cost to employ us and a reasonable administrative fee on top of that. Company owners know quite well what I'm talking about. An employee costs significantly more than their take-home salary. When you include insurance, FICA, 403b matching, and the other things the organization's administration takes care of and that we were now responsible to raise funds for ... I stared at the number, wide-eyed and paralyzed. "All things are possible with God" is easier said as a cliché than lived out in real life. And the number staring back at me, even when divided by 12 (months), was shocking.

Much like the beep of a truck backing up in the distance, the number **8500** kept coming to mind. $8,500 a month seemed somehow achievable. However, there was a gap between that figure and the one Reliant's gross pay required to match our net income needs. So, 8500. Where did that number come from? I felt some assurance from this familiar whisper that God would provide financially in our impending crisis.

God did provide. I was comforted during our Reliant staff training when I remembered my lunch conversation with Mike while eating gyros at Angelo's. Mike was an active member in the church where we had just resigned. When he asked about our future and I told him of our missionary status plans, without hesitation he said, "Sign Kim and me up for $100. We'll be your first supporters."

Another memory that gave me comfort during our time in Orlando was recalling an unexpected phone call I'd taken as I sat with Julie talking at a local coffee shop along the picturesque Chattahoochee River. I had flown to Atlanta to drive her home following her six-week immersive encounter of connecting with God offered through Grace Ministries in Marietta. The outdoor setting was tranquil, the temperature was ideal, but the reality of our rejecting the NDA and the bank check with it weighed heavy on us as we talked. My cell phone rang. I put Aaron, a pastor and peer, on the speaker so Julie could listen in. He wanted to tell us that he had been prompted that morning to commit $50 monthly, and he needed a link to get started. These two memories of God's preemptive provision before our Orlando experience gave us enough confidence to stay the course and complete our orientation with our new mission agency, Reliant.

Reliant gave us an advance to get started with the account for which we were responsible. Having just returned to Columbia from our whirlwind training, we received an invitation from Greg and Terri, dear spiritual friends, to come to their home for dinner. Over dinner, unsolicited and without any prompting from us, they communicated their intention to join our ministry team with financial support. Being the avoidant attachment personality I am, I dismissed myself to their living room, doubled over with uncontrollable sobs, overwhelmed with relief and gratitude, and felt God's presence through their generosity.

All three of these teammates still give faithfully to our ministry so we can do what God has called us to in this season ... *be the mentors to ministry leaders we wish we had had.* These are but three ministry partners of the 75 or so who said yes to our need. Two of our supporters give anonymously. Consistently, our recurring monthly giving average is $8,500 and the gap is made up by special annual gifts, typically given at the end of the year. Now I look back and say of those early days of our fundraising experience, "It wasn't fun, but it wasn't hard." People are so generous. People want to partner financially to get good things done in the world. We have felt so loved. I didn't know how badly I needed the tangible expression of letting people we loved love us back. I would never have ever guessed how secure I now feel getting a paycheck from Jesus through the dozens of His followers who support our mission work "from their own resources" (Luke 8:1-3).

YOUR STORY

The experience described above helped me grow in valuing the kingdom work that gets done in support ministries, often poorly referred to as parachurch ministry. I've recently come to see more clearly the two administrations[2] in kingdom work. They are both embedded within the pages of the New Testament. One is the work of modality (mode), the other sodality (Latin meaning fellowship or fraternity). One is the administration of local synagogues, parishes, and churches. The other is the administration of Jewish brotherhoods, monastic orders, and support ministries.

James, Peter, and the Jerusalem council represent the first administration. Paul and his band of sisters and brothers who discipled the Gentiles represent the second. While local churches prioritize structure, accountability, and unity, associations can prioritize flexibility, effectiveness, and mission. In retrospect, I wish I had seen these two administrations in God's economy sooner and valued the essential work of nonprofits/mission associations more.

In Galatians 2, we read about a conflict in the first century evangelical church. The rabbi Paul (missionary to the non-Jews) is eating bacon and is with his buddies when apostle Peter (missionary to his fellow Jews) shows up for a visit in Galatia. Peter finds out he likes bacon with his pita bread. He likes it a lot until some Jerusalem Church members (modality) show up too. Peter, facing a conundrum, quickly abandons his Christian freedom and reverts to his kosher ways. Paul, seeing his hypocrisy and concerned about the confusion this might cause his non-Jewish new believers, goes toe to toe with Peter and confronts him. Modality and sodality are having what may have been their first fight. Peter sides with the Jerusalem Church mode of operating as soon as that constituency

2   For more information on the "two administrations" read the work of Bob Blincoe (RobertBlincoe.blog) following in the footsteps of Dr. Ralph Winter's address at the 1974 Lausanne Conference on World Evangelization.

shows up. He abandons Paul and the Great Commission when the relational pressure starts to boil.

The reason I'm talking to you about this tension is because it helps explain a critical fracture that became a split in the sad tale of Woodcrest Chapel. And I think it might help you to unpack your past or future experiences too. Navigating the scandal described in this chapter, the church board of directors, the key staff, and a third of the congregation hunkered down to maintain institutional stability (modality).

Other staff members, and a third of the congregation prioritized the mission and the integrity required to fulfill it (sodality). They were willing to risk the short-term pain for the long-term commitment to ethical principles and accountability. Offhandedly, I describe it this way: Some were thinking through the metaphor of "cousins." You don't tattle on your cousin to the authorities. You don't disown your cousin. You don't put the family reunion and peace at risk by telling your cousin he can't come this year and maybe never again.

Others of us viewed ministry through the "ministry partners" lens. We didn't join and serve for friendship. That was an outcome if we could get it, more of an unexpected benefit. Our priority was personal transformation for the sake of others. We were unwilling to harm the mission to save hurt feelings. If you think me being unfair, I ask for an umbrella of mercy. I don't mean to say one side did not value integrity and mission, nor to suggest that the other side devalued stability and unity. What I do mean to say is that when push comes to shove and the conflict gets real, priorities are made, and win-win gets flushed.

As much as I like sounding smart, using big words like modality and sodality, I like being helpful more. You won't navigate a lifetime of kingdom work without facing tension between these two New Testament administrations. As you navigate your own conflicts, I'm hoping you'll glean wisdom from ways I'm learning from mine.

1. How does this idea of two administrations resonate with you? How do the two responses of family or partners help explain conflicts you may be experiencing?
2. What in your world would you get done if you stopped waiting on the faith community you are a part of to give you permission and validation?
3. Meditate on I Corinthians 11 and consider the emphasis on edification as a purpose for gathering.
4. What brewing conflict are you avoiding? Is it a tension to be aware of or a conflict that needs to get solved?

CHAPTER EIGHT

"Write them a letter."

J UST WEEKS BEFORE the start of my high school years, my dad announced it had been decided the daycare would be moving from its current location in the educational wing of the church and into the upstairs portion of the parsonage, which was our home. The new Christian school was expanding and needed the space; the daycare was taking over the parsonage. He attempted to console our shock by adding that our time in the unfinished, cramped downstairs quarters would only be temporary. He and my mom would be looking for a place to move us into while they built their dream home out on the Harrison Lake Road property they had purchased.

I was no stranger to the parsonage basement. It served as my bedroom, roller skating rink, October haunted house, and boxing ring for my brothers and me through the years. What I was a stranger to was having my mom, dad, and invalid grandmother inhabit the limited square footage too! My brothers and I moved into the storage/freezer room while Grandma and my parents took the bedrooms. My mom cooked on a hot plate next to the washer and dryer. The six of us shared the primitive bathroom.

This inconvenient season of living in cramped conditions would merit but a speed bump in my adolescent story were it not for what developed over the next few weeks. My dad, quite unexpectedly, became ill with the sickness that eventually took his life in my sophomore year of college. We didn't move out of our cramped quarters until my senior year of high school, when we moved into a double-wide trailer in a mobile home park nearby. My parents eventually built their dream home, but not until after I'd left.

I recall my mother pleading with my busy pastor father to go to the doctor for help with his nagging cough. He ignored her pleas and before Christmas that year he was admitted into the hospital, diagnosed with congestive heart failure. Doing their best to pastor the bustling church with multiple ministries, they were out of town months at a time for treatment, including an early pacemaker, and recuperation. In the meantime, my siblings cared for Grandma and managed the livestock—a side hustle of Dad's, complete with 40 cows and 100 hogs. This was in addition to my schoolwork and church three times a week. Mind you, this was all happening in the parsonage only 50 yards behind Second Baptist Church in Festus/Crystal City, which featured an auditorium that seated 850, the Twin City Christian School, a Christian bookstore, Living Springs Camp, and a daily radio broadcast, just to name a few.

I describe our home growing up as Grand Central Station. The beauty of that? We weren't bored. The significance that we were doing meaningful work isn't lost on me. We sacrificed for things that mattered. I carry profound respect for the joyful attitude my parents maintained, always modeling a "we can't believe we get to do this for Jesus" posture. BUT ... I would have liked to have been included in the decision-making process that led to these circumstances, asked what I was feeling as I watched my father physically deteriorate, or at least heard, "Wow, this must be hard."

The reason I'm telling you this part of my story is because I'm now explicitly aware of why I care deeply about living space and the safety/security I experience as a result. The home we live in, as I am writing this book, is the safest physical space on earth for me and it is an indisputable testimony to *the power of a whisper*. Here's that story.

My in-laws shared a home with us for 24 years. Together, we lived in two different homes, with "mother-in-law" accommodations, complete with separate kitchens, entrances, etc. For 21 of those years, it was almost ideal. We had more home than we could have afforded on our own. My father-in-law, Richard, was a "fix-it" kind of guy. Pat, my mother-in-law, loved mowing the grass. Our daughters had easy access to their grandparents, and we enjoyed the luxury of having live-in sitters. We could just open a connecting door and Julie had the freedom to go with me for an unexpected pastoral call to the hospital or to intervene in a marriage meltdown.

The last three years were increasingly more of a challenge. Caring for Richard and Pat exceeded our capacity to keep them, and us, safe. Our interventions started including instructions such as: "We don't hit each other in this house!" "Because you threatened Mom, we're going to have to take your guns," and "You can't treat the visiting nurses that way."

In the summer of 2017, Julie and I agreed we could no longer keep doing things this way and some kind of transition was necessary. We were doing our best to get them what they needed, and it was no longer working. When we sat down to discuss other possibilities with them, they *flipped their lids*. "You'll carry us out in handcuffs," they responded. "We're going to consult an attorney," they threatened. Within days, they announced that their son, Julie's brother, was going to take over their care and was coming to move them into a rented house near his residence in another city.

Those who care for aging parents know in their bones the toll this was taking on Julie. Her years of doing her best to honor her parents, going with them to visit their doctors, enforcing it when Richard was told he could no longer drive, check their prescriptions, and include them in family events was now being reciprocated with hostility, distance, and financial consequences. As relationally gut-wrenching as all this was, Julie barely had time to process. We had a house with more room than we needed and it was more than we could afford on our own.

I'm told she and Jesus had a long talk one morning while all this was happening around us. What they discussed in detail, I don't know, but what I do know is she told me later that day, "I don't have to live in this house. Let's go find one together where we can start a new season of our faith adventure." A trait I've admired in her all these years was coming to fruition once again. She and Jesus were working stuff out and she was bringing her full self into whatever was next.

I, on the other hand, was a simmering volcano over the situation. My inadequacy in fixing the situation and feeling even more dismayed by my in-laws' lack of regard for our reality was crushing. Their unwillingness to even discuss options for their future was overwhelming. My nervous system was overwhelmed when

I opened the Realtor.com app with one hand while holding an Andy's frozen custard in the other.

Isn't God good to meet us, even in our unregulated, comfort-food ways?

I consulted the app to see if an affordable home might be available in the neighborhood just north of the Stephens Lake area where I was sitting. I recalled liking that drive past the golf course and the neighborhood was conveniently located near downtown Columbia with its medical facilities, parks, restaurants, and retail outlets. As soon as I opened the app, a brick house with a beautiful front door, a screened-in porch, a remodeled interior, and even a trash compactor appeared on the screen. Who but God knew I needed a trash compactor?!

From the moment we walked through the front door at the showing, I felt safe. I had never experienced that feeling like I did that day and every day since. I believe with all my heart it was a kiss of affection from our Father, giving me a gift to help heal my soul and my body's longing for space where I could feel *home*. It was a far cry from past lodgings: the parsonage, the unfinished basement, dorm rooms, seminary apartments, or even homes we owned and shared with in-laws. I trust you are picking up what I'm laying down. I don't regret any of those decisions and those physical spaces were perfect for those seasons. But there was another season coming I didn't even know I needed. In that season, I would find myself in a home where I could mentor, write, be neighborly, host grandkids, and reflect on the healing grace[1] this home provides.

---

1   In case you are wondering, Julie now finds the same solace in our home as I do. It grew on her as she gave it her creative touch. She even named it... and a framed needlepoint our daughter Miriam made for us sits prominently as a reminder. The name? "Healing Grace."

Though reeling from yet another transition, Julie agreed it would be a good house. We thought it ironic that I had found this house and was so intent on purchasing it. Aesthetics are not normally my forte and attention to our living conditions was a rather latent quality. An unfinished basement had been my starting point. Shared space had been my experience. Being happy wherever was in my bones. Choosing where I wanted to live? This was new for me, and I admitted I wanted it bad. That's risky when it comes to real estate. You're not supposed to let yourself get too excited. A lot can go wrong.

Much to my disappointment, it was decided we would sleep on it while we considered our offer. We had scheduled a meeting with our real estate agent the next morning to discuss the details and potential offer to purchase the house. That night I had a thought that was not my thought. Where did that come from, I wondered? It's true I have had enough of these thoughts at this point in my life to know the answer to that question. I was again encountering the power of a whisper, a divine voice offering instruction for a specific situation we found ourselves in.

I heard four words: **"Write them a letter."** Without hesitation I promptly opened my Chromebook and typed this letter to the owners of the home.

August 17, 2017

To the family of Jim (and Julia) King:
I want you to know my intentions for buying your home. My wife, Julie, and I have shared a home with an in-law apartment with her parents for the past 24 years, with

a commitment to care for them in the home as long as we could. Their physical care now exceeds our capacity, and they will be moving out on or before September 1. Sparing you details, we have decided to make our own transition and start new memories elsewhere in Columbia. We are busy getting our house listed and on the market as soon as possible. We are hopeful about our prospects to sell quickly, but as you know... no guarantees.

The prospects of moving closer to downtown and near Stephens Lake Park are exciting, especially as new grandparents. Who knows, we might even join the country club (nearby)!

I know this expression of intention is unorthodox, but I felt led to do so. I know what it's like to wonder if a house will ever sell or if the people who buy it will love it like you do. Maybe I'm feeling sentimental about the prospects of selling this one. Jim King's reputation in the community is admirable. I had the privilege of meeting him once outside of the high school while he was principal. My daughter Hannah works at RBHS [Rock Bridge High School] in the front office. We are sad with you for his passing. His obituary was fitting of his legacy. If we are able to negotiate a contract, I'm hoping we can hear the stories that home can tell.

Just wanted you to know.
Rod Casey

David, our long-time friend and Realtor, lovingly chided me for insisting we include a *forever-home letter* with the offer we were sending to their Realtor. I'm now aware writing these types of sentimental letters to sellers is somewhat common, but I assure you I knew nothing of it at the time. All I knew is, I had been prompted by that good gift Jesus promised us, the Holy Spirit, to do so, and I did.

You can imagine my shock/not shock when their Realtor told us unsolicited at the closing what the deciding factor was in the sellers accepting our offer instead of the others. Care to guess? It was the letter ... the letter prompted by the power of a whisper.

YOUR STORY

We honor our parents by telling the truth. The truth is, my in-laws didn't finish well, and aging can't explain away what I'm talking about. Certainly, they had many good qualities. Their investment in kingdom purposes through their "Heart to Heart Bookstore" is admirable. Their vengeful response to our limited capacity to care for them any further is heartbreaking.

I care about finishing well. I care about you finishing well. I care about you and me turning 73, 83, or 93 and still being the life of the kingdom party. Neither age nor suffering should be excuses for becoming selfish and demanding. No believers get a pass to not act Christianly; not brides on their wedding day, not pastors who have been hurt, not retirees forced out of a job, not even turning 21 gives us permission to quit modeling Jesus.

It matters a lot that as godly people, we do not embarrass our families, our churches, ourselves by checking out on the Jesus

Way and choosing to live in an ungodly way. Becoming bitter is easy. We can do that. Not becoming increasingly bitter, selfish, and purposeless at any age—we need help with that.

During my early ministry years at Dallas Seminary, I became somewhat obsessed with the question of how to live a virtuous life. Put simply, I didn't want to be the next Jim Bakker, Jimmy Swaggart, Frank Tillapaugh, or Gordon MacDonald. These were the public ministry scandals of the 1980s. The Gordon MacDonald debacle hit closest to home because I had heard him preach in DTS chapel and been positively impacted by his book, "Ordering Your Private World." His response to discipline and subsequent restoration, culminating in a book entitled, "Rebuilding Your Broken World," is a testimony to grace, but not to be emulated. It's tragic and I didn't want to be a casualty or a cause of great consequence.

This side of heaven, all sin is not the same, despite the cliché. There is a weight of consequence related to fraud, illicit sexual activity, teaching heresy, acts of revenge, etc. But why does it happen and how can I avoid it? These were burning questions for me in my early years.

The answer, for me, came in the form of a resource entitled, "Overcoming the Dark Side of Leadership" (Baker Books, 2007, 256 p.) by Dr. Sam Rima and Gary McIntosh. I've joked through the years that Sam is the first author I ever stalked. I called the church he was pastoring at the time in Nebraska, and the church secretary gave me his home phone number. When I called that number, his wife gave Sam the phone and a ministry partnership began.[2]

This book was Dr. Rima's published Doctor of Ministry project from Talbot School of Theology. In it, he introduced me to the five personality dysfunctions ministry leaders needed to know and address to avoid becoming a casualty. The point of Sam's project and the answers I was seeking were this ... people don't commit gross sin in one act; they deny and ignore the smaller stuff that needs attention. They won't admit the negative coping mechanisms that they use to dull the unmet needs and traumatic experiences of their past.

The five personality dysfunctions Dr. Rima describes are these:

1. **The Compulsive Leader (103-109):** "Compulsive in a leadership context describes the need to maintain absolute order" (105). The compulsive leader has trouble with delegation, tending toward workaholism. They are conscientious but moralistic and may become judgmental. They are conscious of their status, looking both for approval and reassurance from others, yet leaning toward anger and rebellion on the inside. The compulsive leader in the church setting relies upon administration and organization as the safety net for their fears of losing control, whether of staff, their board, or the ministry of the church. Moses is an example of the tendencies toward control seen in the compulsive leader.

2   We brought Dr. Rima to central Missouri shortly thereafter for a daylong workshop on the material. We employed his book as required reading for church membership. Later, Sam became the director of the doctoral program at Bethel Seminary, St. Paul, and invited me to join the faculty as an adjunct professor. I'm indebted to Sam's investment in me through both his writing and his invitation to teach.

2. **The Narcissistic Leader (111-118):** "For the narcissistic leader ... the world revolves on the axis of self, and all other people and issues closely orbit them as they get caught in the strong gravitational pull of the narcissist's self-absorption" (115). Leaders with this dark side tend to overestimate their own achievements and abilities while stubbornly refusing to recognize the quality and value of the same in others" (115). They are often driven by unmet needs for admiration toward the pursuit of success and can be simultaneously over-inflated in their sense of importance and deeply insecure. In the church setting, the narcissistic leader will promote themselves, their endeavors and their gifts aggressively, and thereby make themselves seem like an essential piece of everything without which nothing could possibly succeed. Solomon is an example of the tendencies toward self-obsession in the narcissistic leader.

3. **The Paranoid Leader (119-126):** "Paranoid leaders are desperately afraid of anything or anyone, whether real or imagined, they perceive to have even the remotest potential of undermining their leadership and stealing away the limelight" (122-123). Oftentimes, paranoid leaders overreact to criticism, guess at others' motives, and rigorously root out those who seem to be against them. The paranoid leader in the church will keep anyone else from preaching or doing anything they can to keep their board from meeting without them. Saul, the first king of Israel, is an example of the tendencies toward suspicion seen in the paranoid leader.

4. **The Codependent Leader (127-138):** Codependency is "an emotional, psychological, and behavioral condition that develops as a result of an individual's prolonged exposure to, and practice of, a set of oppressive rules—rules that

prevent the open expression of feeling as well as the direct discussion of personal and interpersonal problems" (133). Codependent people compulsively worry about the feelings of other people, even taking responsibility for others' actions and emotions, while often being out of touch with their own emotions. Codependents are often reactive instead of proactive. "Ministry and Christian service organizations provide the perfect environment for a leader to focus on others to the exclusion of self. This often results in the codependent pastor or leader's failure to care for himself, producing burnout and other debilitating maladies" (136). Samson is an example of the tendencies toward emotional and relational stunting experienced with the codependent leader.

5. **The Passive-Aggressive Leader (139-146):** "Passive-aggressive leaders have a tendency to resist demands to adequately perform tasks," (140) oftentimes based on a fear of failure. The passive-aggressive leader may have outbursts of intense emotions, manifest various forms of impulsiveness, and can become perennial complainers. In the church setting, passive-aggressive leaders radiate edgy irritability, often complaining about their workload, the people they work with, and the sort of things they must do. They make impulsive decisions, while also procrastinating essential tasks, both of which can alienate congregants and volunteers from them. Jonah is an example of the tendencies toward emotional outbursts and impulsiveness often seen in passive-aggressive leaders.

You may be tempted to argue the home you grew up in wasn't dysfunctional. "I had great parents," you say. I hear you. But that's kind of the point I'm trying to make. I grew up in a parsonage behind the church. The stress in our home could be considered mild and my parents' service in the work of the church admired. They did their work with joy. But that doesn't translate into me feeling only 62% abandoned by my father. No, I felt neglected the only way emotions come: a full on 100. I was feeling invisible to my pastor/father, but other adults assumed I was doing fine. My school and church youth group peers got attention I longed for. They came from moderate or severely dysfunctional families. Their need was obvious. But since I was a good kid from a model home, they wrongly assumed I wasn't struggling. Or if they did, they didn't know how to intervene.

My point is not to throw my parents under the bus or minimize the amazing adults who cared deeply for me. My point is the way I survived, manifested in me through codependency and over-responsibility. Hard work and "knowing what to do" not only gave me my own accolades and ministry advancement, but those same traits caused pain for my wife and daughters. When I didn't know what to do, I froze, and I mean that in the "fight, flight, or freeze" kind of way. While I cared about, had awareness of, and sought help with my shadow sides of codependency and paranoia, what was left unprocessed still created harm for those around me. Dealing with my default survival strategies by making the implicit (unspoken stories of my past) explicit (telling these stories for the purpose of healing) was needed, and more work is still ahead. Telling the truth about our parents and ourselves is a lifelong work needed if we are to finish well. I'm committed to doing that hard work. How about you?

1. Take the assessment Sam offers at no charge to determine your own dysfunctional vulnerability at Darksideprofile.com.

2. Ask family members and spiritual friends to help you see what you don't through the vocabulary of the results of your assessment.
3. Get a copy of the book or audiobook and commit to a lifetime of processing the shadow side(s) of your leadership qualities.
4. Meditate on the truth of your identity in Christ (II Corinthians 5:17). We are not our flesh patterns (coping mechanisms). Yet, we carry around this "body of death" (Romans 7:24) and yield the members of our soul to precepts and practices that bring us to full maturity in Him (Ephesians 3:14-21).

CHAPTER NINE

"How do you want to do it?"

——————

THE METHOD OF COMPENSATION for information is to charge a fee for it. This is nearly universal in Western society. When we attend a conference, go to a concert, or take a course, we pay for it. Substack and podcasts are free, but if you want the rest of the creator's content, you become a paid subscriber or a patron. We expect to pay for it. It's the way the world works. There is a predetermined amount where the consumer decides whether they think the value of the experience will be worth the cost. This kind of monetization for resources is common.

By contrast, our Theological Education Initiative of Central Missouri gives her resources away for free and asks those who believe in it or benefit from it to support her through freewill offerings. Special and recurring monthly donations fuel the economic engine that has allowed our missional flywheel to keep spinning since its nonprofit incorporation in 2012. "There's no cost for what you're about to experience, but it's not free," I say to those attending one of our lectures or benefitting from any of our services. "It's provided by individuals and churches who make investments in you and your continuing education. If you can help with any amount, we'd be grateful."

Hear me on this. I'm not making any value statements, nor do I judge the motivations of those who monetize developing leaders for ministry. In fact, my adjunct teaching and writing, focused on teaching and preaching, modestly benefit from this model. I'm undecided as I write these stories about how this resource you hold will be distributed and paid for. Culturally speaking, I'm aware that people may value something more if they pay for it. If there's no charge, it may be assumed that it's worth nothing. Western culture is conditioned to think about education this way, so it somehow seems un-American to do it differently.

I don't want to do the work we do with theological education that way. I haven't always been as confident about this as I am now. Instead, I felt tortured by this question in the early years of TEI's existence. The way it got settled for me was through the power of a whisper.

It was a Sunday morning, and I was driving across town to attend the morning service where our visiting lecturer was speaking. Apologist and author Mike Licona masterfully communicated his apologetic for the reliability of the gospels during the Friday evening and Saturday morning lectures we hosted in the Parkade Center. While driving, I wrestled with the list of area ministry leaders who hadn't come instead of celebrating those who did. I often feel discouraged following these events, focusing more on who needed them, any others who might have otherwise benefited from them, and those who said they were coming but failed to show up. I scold myself for having these feelings, then remind myself obsessing over those who didn't attend minimizes the ones who did, and the beat goes on, and on, and on.

I awakened Sunday morning, this dance still in my head, when I recalled something our visiting scholar had said to me on the day of the conference. He told me that at nearly all the events where he's invited to present his scholarship, the attendees are charged an event fee of $39, $59, $99, or more. He expressed surprise at our providing the TEI event at no cost, and if there might be benefits to monetizing the seminar instead.

This and more were swirling in my mind as I drove to the final installment of our theology weekend. Amid this mixed bag of emotions, rationalization, and potential vows of what I would or wouldn't do, I asked Father if he had a perspective. The thought that immediately materialized that I knew didn't originate from me was simply this, **"How do you want to do it?"**

How do I want to do it? I ask the Creator of all things, the omnipotent One, He who knows the beginning from the end, and God asks me what I want to do? Yes, that very God!

"I like the way we do it," I recall saying out loud. "I don't want under-resourced leaders to not come because they can't afford it and are too embarrassed to ask for a scholarship." My argument continued, "I don't want to deal with people who walk away thinking it wasn't worth what they paid for it and wishing they could get a refund. I like how we're doing it, Father."

The calm my spirit experienced in that moment was the Father's affirmation that he liked what I liked. And that was that.

This account underscored for me the theological truth of what it means to co-create with God. Or as my dad used to say to it, "Get up and do something, even if you do it wrong." See a need and meet that need. Make a difference. Leave your world better than you found it.

My wife believes in her core that personal growth is in our story. One such story from my past takes place when I interrupted my dad's reading of the Bible during breakfast to ask him what and why *circumcision* was in the Bible. My brothers were spitting food and splitting their sides in laughter. My pastor father mumbled something about cutting the way we cut the mountain oysters off cows and pigs and concluded with an "Ask your mother."

I now know I felt shame, embarrassed for asking a question that evoked such awkwardness. But what I did with that shame wasn't to project it on myself as if I should have known better than to ask that question, but to project it onto my family instead. What I experienced was more like, "I didn't make up these rules. You're the one reading the Bible. That's what **it** says and if you can't explain circumcision any better than that, shame on you!" And somewhere deep inside I know I resolved that someday I was going to figure out why the Old Testament was so bloody, brutal, and barbaric and be able to explain it to a kid like me.

At the heart of my vocational contribution to this world I've inhabited is the need to make hard-to-understand things about God and His Word more accessible. It is both humbling and rewarding to summarize my contribution to a single motivation. But when I do, it sounds like this: "I'm helping my under-resourced parents do meaningful ministry work in ways that would have had even greater benefit for me and the others they served." Other than my mom, who was the better Bible student and theologian than anybody in my younger world, most of my big questions were met with a "We believe in believing and you sure ask hard questions, Rod." I found their lives compelling, and their joy was contagious, but when it came to *apologetic* reasons for why we believe what we believe, I felt shame as a kid for thinking faith should be grounded in knowledge.

TEI was incorporated in 2012, but its beginnings were birthed 24 years earlier. Central Missouri had everything I could ever want—college gamedays, international flair, a small-town vibe, good schools for my kids, and evangelical momentum I wanted to help foster. What it didn't have was something I had come to highly value during our time in Dallas: a theological reference library and lunch lecture discussions. I couldn't afford the expensive Bible commentaries (everything was hard copy back then) while pursuing my degree, and we certainly couldn't afford them on our church-planting and pioneering salary. I often thought, it shouldn't be this hard or expensive to get these life-changing resources. Somebody ought to do something about that. And in this little part of the planet, that somebody turns out to be me.

TEI is a partner organization to the Consortium of Christian Study Centers. While their focus is the preservation of orthodox faith solely on secular campuses, our commitment is to the broader faith community. Our commitment to minority, rural, support ministries (for example, Young Life), and of course, to our local campus staff sets us apart. I like to describe it as a not-for-profit answer to the need for a non-denominational evangelical seminary in our area.

Our vision is healthier faith communities. Our mission is to provide theological, philosophical, and practical resources to under-resourced ministry leaders. Our strategy is to provide a historically evangelical reference library, lectures with visiting scholars, financial scholarships for further educational experiences, and a three-year orientation to theological studies through our Emerging Church Leadership Institute.

TEI's primary target is not for those already educated. Ministry leaders who have an accredited theological degree are welcome to participate, of course, but they typically have access to what they need through denominational or digital resources available to them.

Our heartbeat is for those faith community leaders who don't know where to start, who don't know who to ask, couldn't afford it if they did, and want to be able to answer the hard questions a middle schooler may ask them in Sunday School next week. That's why "How do you want to do it?" was my default response that day as I drove across town. I long to drag the treasures of the theological academy out onto the front lawn for anybody willing to access them, along with a "for free" sign clearly displayed.

My experience with the power of this whisper—"How do you want to do it?"—ought not become a vow. If we're not mindful, experiences become vows, and vows become strongholds. If the future of TEI includes some modest fees for the resources she provides, so be it. Otherwise, the vow of "We've always done it this way" becomes a stronghold that chokes the discernment process needed for leaders in a new season.

Discernment is what I hope you hear. My unique experiences, my personal longings, my relationship with God—these factors and more are the ingredients for enthusiastic (en-theos, in-God) living. That's the reason I don't quite know yet whether TEI will outlast me. I don't wish for it to become institutionalized if that means it lives in strongholds rooted in vows that drift from meeting the need for which it was founded. A 10-year-old kid like me with big questions and big feelings sitting at a breakfast table hearing the Bible read wants to hear instead: "That's a great question. Thank you for asking. And the rest of you shouldn't be laughing. I don't know the answer, but I know a place nearby (TEI) that can help, and it won't cost us anything to find out. I'll get back to you. How does that sound?" The 10-year-old me smiles and responds, "That would be solid!"

YOUR STORY

How do you want to do it? What do you want to do?

These two questions often cause those I mentor to recoil when asked. I can feel their well-intentioned resistance in the answers they give, "Do you mean what is God's will for my life?" or "Do you mean what do my parents, teachers, or peers think I should do?" or "I assume you mean what am I good at?" After we've sat together with that question for a while, they often drop their shoulders and, with a sigh, conclude, "I don't know what I want to do."

Even the question "How do you want to do it?" may seem counterintuitive to well-meaning believers, especially to younger followers of Jesus. Our struggle with the emotion of shame telling us that there is something foundationally wrong with us leaves us wanting certainty. "If only God would tell me what He wants me to do!" we lament.

Of course, you believe that I believe in God's Providence. It should be obvious I believe God can give clarity in some decision-making processes. That is what this book is about—12 of those experiences where I've encountered the power of a personal whisper from God. But there have been a lot of other decisions, even embedded in these 12, where I have exercised human agency, all the while trusting that His Spirit is in my spirit and trusting that His will is getting done.

Theologically speaking, we call this co-creating. We are taking up our part in "ruling and subduing" on earth in ways like what God, with heavenly beings, does in heaven. From the early pages of Scripture, we see our Creator Father letting the created Ish (man) name the animals. Even the strong companion (ezer kenegdo) he let Adam name, and he called her Ishah (woman). It made sense to Adam because she was from a part of him. God gave them freedom to eat freely from any tree in the garden except one. That tree represented trying to live outside of their human capacity, the responsibility to determine what was right or wrong alone. In Genesis 15:8 Abram asks YHWH to give him certainty about the future of the land. In return, God gives him a covenant promise that it will get done.

Don't get me wrong. There is a beauty in asking what God wants done. That is an essential posture for discerning. Otherwise, we are tempted to answer the questions from a posture of what will be most effective? What will give us more influence? What *should*

be done? Effectiveness, more influence, and obligation are vari-
ables in the equation of a God-honoring decision, but they need
to take a backseat to significance, character, and invitation. It may
be un-American to choose consistency over volume, character
over power, or freedom instead of overworking. But it is the way
of Jesus.

It has been told that Dallas Willard said when he had a decision
to make, he asked God for "His Thoughts" for three days. If he
had not experienced anything during this discernment process, he
then decided and trusted Sovereignty to work it all out.

This may be a revolutionary thought for you to consider: What if
you keep asking God what He wants you to do and He is asking
you in return, "How do you want to do it? What do you want to
do?" Can you move without certainty? Can you discipline your
doubts? Will you let your God-given deepest longings free? Will
you risk embarrassment? Can you envision "failure" and keep
your identity in Christ intact?

I'll go first. These questions are the stuff my experiences are made
of. How about you? How do you want to do it? What do you want
to do? Come on, admit it. Say it. Risk it. Do it. You've heard the
cliché "God can't steer a parked car?" Now there's a cliché with
wisdom, worthy of repeating.

1. What do you think about this phrase? "Some things are worth
    doing poorly."
2. What role is shame playing in your feeling stuck and undecid-
    ed about your future?

3. Meditate on Genesis 15. What certainty is God asking you to forfeit in trusting Him?

4. Pray this prayer... *"Oh Lord, what have I to offer my world that might be of help to others? I see little more to offer than my insecurity, my shame, and my fear of rejection.*

5. Let me see something greater in me, my Creator Father. Let me see the beauty, the giftings, the desires, the longings, the contributions that You entrusted in me before the woundedness distorted my ability to see them. Through me, let me be a blessing to others in ways I alone cannot."

CHAPTER TEN

"You could do that."

———

URING MY EMPLOYMENT at the Stadium McDonald's, I
had a daily tasks list: empty the cooking oil fryers, clean
the filthy restrooms, sort the rotten tomatoes from the
good ones, wash miles of windows, and of course, pick up any
trash tossed within a block of the restaurant. A block covers a
lot of black top and grass, but that's what the founder, Ray Kroc,
demanded. When I finally left that job, I vowed never to "do tomatoes" or pick up someone else's litter again. Ever.

Be careful what you vow.

Vows will come back to bite you in the butt. That's what happened
to me the day I drove into the church parking lot dressed in my
khaki pants and a button-down collared shirt instead of a striped,
blue uniform with the golden arches stitched into the pocket.
Eight years after seminary, I landed my first traditional staff role
with a job description somebody else wrote. At last, I would know
what it was like to have a reliable paycheck from a church, even if
it only totaled $24,000 a year. I was excited to pastor and disciple
people eager to apprentice with Jesus. What I didn't want was to
sort any more rotten tomatoes. Check.

Or pick up candy bar wrappers that I hadn't thrown on the ground.

But there it was, as I stepped out of my car to enter the building: a half-eaten banana with a bruised peel. As if on cue, I said to myself, "I don't do tomatoes and I don't pick up litter. You think somebody would do something about that! Doesn't this operation have a janitor?" No sooner had the thought crossed my mind, than I felt a spiritual correction. "How about you, big boy? You were trained in the McClean system. You've got this!"

I don't believe everyone is obligated to do everything that needs doing. There are tasks we don't see that others notice. Some folks get paid to do things and may very well enjoy doing them. Yet, there are menial tasks, small things unique to our story that God invites us to share in. These things keep us grounded. They remind us of our Example as He washed His followers' feet.

Picking up litter most people step over is a gentle reminder of my place in the cultural mandate of Genesis. Doing my part in creation care isn't only about supporting my family and mentoring next generation ministry leaders. Bending down to pick up a crushed beer can, collecting the plastic grocery bags to take to the food bank, and giving a pint of blood every eight weeks or so—these are Christian formation practices I find good for my soul.

Over the years, picking up litter has become my regular spiritual practice. I remind myself this is my Father's world, and He appreciates my efforts to keep it clean. I don't have to sort rotten tomatoes from the good ones, and I can be grateful for that. I'm pretty good about staying around to stack a few chairs after a neighborhood potluck. I do my part. That's why I was a reluctant participant in another seemingly small task asked of me a couple of years ago.

There I was, minding my own business and listening to an OnScript podcast, when it happened. On days that are too cold to walk outside, I drive across town to join the Columbia Mall Walkers. It was a Friday morning, and I wanted to complete two full loops around the mall before heading over to our Study Center to fine-tune the sermon for Sunday. I was filling the pulpit as the guest speaker for a church in our community. But first, two loops.

I nearly collided with a sign in the mall's atrium and immediately looked up. It was strategically placed in the atrium path to grab the public's attention, and it certainly got mine. It read simply, "Blood Drive Today." My brain was busily digesting the biblical scholarship from the podcast when I heard it, not with my body's ears, but my internal ears. (I was tempted to say my "innie" for all the *Severance* TV show fans out there. I resisted.) The thought wasn't audible—they never have been—but loud enough to drown out the other thoughts inside my head. **"You could do that."** Plain and simple.

"Do what?" I may have said it out loud. I had enough wits about me to know donating blood is a good thing. It saves lives. Hospitals need it. People depend on it for life-sustaining recovery from injuries or disease. I thought it important for people to sacrifice an hour or so from time to time to endure having a needle stuck in their arm and give a pint for a worthy cause. It just never occurred to me to do it until that moment when I had yet another unexpected encounter with a Holy Spirit, this time whispering, "You could do that."

This experience matters because it represents even seemingly small things the Spirit may prompt us to do. I am often prone to dismiss everyday opportunities with "Somebody else will get that," or "They probably don't want my help anyway." I recall a time recently when I sensed a leading to help a neighbor lift a rented bounce house into the back of his pickup truck. I talked myself out of it. Same Spirit. I ignored the leading. I regret it, wondering even now what possible adventure I might have missed.

It took me another full lap shuffling along the mall hallways before I made my way to the technicians, raised my sleeve and had a nurse prick my finger and stick a needle in my arm. After she drew the pint of blood, I was rewarded with a package of Oreo cookies. I do love any excuse to eat cookies.

My working definition of the character trait of humility is having an accurate picture of who God created me to be. To think less of myself is a tall order. But thinking more of myself than is healthy is my greater temptation. Inconvenient acts of service, like those I've described above, remind me of my created place in this part of the planet.

I know there's always more personal formation needed because I'm often guilty of hoping someone will see me doing one of these small tasks. Perhaps, I think to myself, if they see me donating blood or taking a Cheetos bag to the trash receptacle, they'll tell their friends, "I saw Pastor Rod today, and guess what he was doing?" Then there'll be an "ooo" or "aahhh" and an "Isn't he something." I've grown in my capacity to have mixed motives. I'm able to celebrate motivations in me that remind me I'm headed to the ground before long and hoping my part of the cemetery is clean. Unless the Lord returns first, of course, which is a claim we dispensationalists must add. It's in our DNA.

In all seriousness, there is a freedom I experienced during my McDonald's years that I want to remember. It's this: My identity is in Jesus, not in titles or outcomes. It was good for me to be invisible to many in the community whenever I stepped into that uniform with a maroon hat, broom in hand. In that defining decade of my 20s, as a recent graduate of a respected graduate school with a four-year degree in theology, I thought I was kind of a big deal, and Columbia should be glad to have me. Turns out, becoming a maintenance man at Mickey D's became the very lesson I needed, especially when those who failed to acknowledge me holding the door for them were too often, I soon discovered, leaders in their faith communities.

"Too big for your britches," Mom used to call it. "Don't forget whose little boy you are," she also said. She meant I belonged to her and Jesus, in case you are wondering. I don't know what so-called small things the Spirit may ask of you, but you will find me donating blood, picking up some litter, and hauling grocery bags into the food bank. I can do that.

Snap! Somebody just let their dog poop in our driveway and didn't pick it up. Somebody ought to do something about that.

YOUR STORY

Small things matter. Your contribution matters. Your seemingly small contribution matters a lot to someone(s) and you are a terrible judge of its value. That's why you can't ever retire.

You heard me. Resist planning for it, celebrating it, or waiting for it. I don't mean there won't come a day when our bills are paid from income we receive from Social Security, pension(s), and our 401ks. That's fine. I'm talking about retiring from what you uniquely contribute to your world and instead become an entitled brat, waking up self-absorbed, expecting to be catered to, or saying, "I've done my part; it's somebody else's turn?" I forbid it.

Getting your mind around how you contribute to your world is a lifelong process. Throughout your life, you will likely talk about it in a variety of ways, but at the core there is a common theme. For me, as best I understand it, it is about being the mentor I wish I'd had. You've heard about this repeatedly throughout this book. I want to be the mentor I wish my dad would have had. I want to be the academic mentor in pastoral ministry that some seminary professors were to me. I feel called to pastor younger ministry-minded women and men. I want to be president of their fan clubs. I want to put gospel ointment on their service wounds. I want to grow old with Julie supporting our two girls, their husbands, and their children. Retire? No thank you.

My oldest brother, Randy, was a model of aging well. If you asked him if you could borrow his truck, for example, he would tell you it wasn't his to loan. "I gave it to God," he would say. "I'm confident He'd be delighted for you to use it." He used the Dave Ramsey cliché when you asked how he was doing. "Better than I deserve!" was his guaranteed comeback. His reputation is legendary in our hometown for getting waitstaff to give him the check of people he knew sitting at tables nearby. He relished the thought of their surprise after he left that their meal was already paid for. Beyond his regular charitable giving commitments, Randy kept a monthly sum of $300 to meet someone's need. On more than one occasion, I was the needy one. That's the testimony of my two daughters as well. When he died in the spring of 2024, he had come alongside a struggling food bank, the Jefferson County Rescue Mission, and, as its director, helped revitalize it. When he couldn't get out of bed any longer, people came to his living room bedside to hear a lame joke, talk about how they were struggling, and let their Pastor Randy pray for them one last time.

A Scripture that reminds us to not look down on small things is Zechariah 4:10. The New Living Translation reads: "Do not despise these small beginnings, for the Lord rejoices to see the work begin." The context surrounds the frail and faltering work of the exiled people returning from Babylon to rebuild Solomon's temple under Zerubbabel, along with the spiritual oversight of Haggai and Zechariah. Even the hanging of a plumb line to get a straight wall was celebrated. No act when motivated by a heart of love was too small.

For me, it can be as simple as a text of encouragement, filling out a reference letter to an academic institution, hosting a theological lecture, or sharing my experiences through writing. Such things are the culmination of the various seasons of my life. Oh, and donating blood. And picking up litter. And playing with dolls with my granddaughters or catching a football with my grandsons. Why would I ever retire from that? I won't, by God's grace!

1. Do you think every decade of your life could be better than the one before? Why or why not?
2. Consider how you are currently contributing to your world. How does what you do matter? What gets done because of the work you do, whether paid or as a volunteer?
3. Locate the idea of "retirement" in the Bible. Sit with the implications of that for you and your future.

4. If you're 50 years old or above, read "Aging Matters: Finding Your Calling for the Rest of You're Life" (R. Paul Stevens, Eerdmans Publishing, 2016, 199 pp.) Seriously, get it. Chapter 5 on "The Vices of Aging" regarding the seven deadly sins of seniors is worth the price of the book. In fact, read it first and then apologize to a millennial if you've called them entitled.

CHAPTER ELEVEN

"Money follows mission."

—————

'M A MOMMA'S BOY. As the youngest of five, I experienced Mom's sole attention when my siblings went off for school. I experienced her care and attention in meaningful ways through my primary years, and for that I'm grateful. During my adolescence, I felt invisible, and for that I'm sad. Her mother, in need of constant care, came to live with us just as the faith community my parents led grew exponentially. These two things, coupled with my father's medical diagnosis, consumed her. Even so, I respected my mother and when she spoke, I listened. It was different with Dad. I respected the fact that my dad was respected. But for Mom, it was nothing but mad respect, as the kids like to say.

Mom was not flawless. I should tell you her feet were firmly planted on the ground. Characteristic of women navigating her "Leave it to Beaver" world, Mom worked to meet everyone's expectations, even if it meant sacrificing her health, and insisted her children join her in unreasonable sacrifices to meet ministry's demands. Mom lived through the Great Depression and World War II. She loathed her father's excessive drinking. She credited her mother (Bessie Mae) with keeping her and her sisters fed and protecting them from their father's abusive ways. I'm guessing all these things were a driving force behind her penchant for overwork.

"Elbow grease" were words she said often during our Saturday chores.

Our pastor's family home was the definition of boundaryless. The telephone, with its tightly wound ten-foot cord, was always answered and the doorbell never ignored. Every church member or community need was urgent, and we kids were "happy to help," even if we weren't! "You've got the same clothes to get glad in that you got mad in," she would tell us.

Mom's default response was to spiritualize any emotional issue. She washed my mouth out with soap for saying "Geez." She really did that to me, dadgummit. I told you she had her flaws. She certainly had her share of flaws, but my admiration for the woman I remember far outweighs any of them. Plus, time is a gift that helps us reinterpret our hurt; not to excuse it, but to explain it.

I respected Mom's love for learning. Christian radio played in the background most of the day as she worked taking phone calls, preparing meals and keeping the parsonage white-glove clean. Radio programs with the Bible teachings of J. Vernon McGee, Woodrow Kroll, Warren Wiersbe, Martin DeHaan, and Lester Roloff, among others, exposited truth treasures through the air waves and from the stereo console of our family room.

Mom became an apprentice of Jesus in her late 20s, when she was already a mother of three. Mrs. Craig, a neighbor in Baytown, Texas, discipled my mother over coffee, while their kids played nearby. At that time, my dad was a roughneck (pipefitter) working offshore on oil rigs. It was a dangerous job and paid good money.

My dad shocked Mom the day he announced his desire to attend a three-year Bible school in Tennessee and become a preacher. My mother told him, "You go right ahead, but me and the kiddos are staying right here!" When she asked Mrs. Craig what she should do about her husband's potential career shift, Mrs. Craig wisely told her to lock herself in the bathroom and ask Jesus about it. When she finished her come-to-Jesus meeting, she said to her husband, and I'm quoting her, "Gene Casey, if you're following Jesus, I'll follow you into the ministry. If you're not following Jesus, I'm going to kill you." In some sense, she didn't have to; ministry did. My parents both worked themselves to death in their early 50s doing what they loved.

I respect my mom for the way she cared about the English language. She sat with The Living Bible paraphrase in her lap, though her husband preached from the classic King James version. "My brother and me, not my brother and I," she would correct when I misspoke the direct object of the verb. I'm sure my own value for clarity and relevance in communication are rooted in her desire for saying things well.

I fondly remember her taking my questions seriously. I sometimes muse that I'm still persuaded by a premillennial, dispensational eschatology because that's what my first professor of theology, Mrs. M. Joyce Casey, taught me at our dining room table, illustrated with an end-times diagram on paper. And yes, it reflected the pre-tribulation rapture view.

I took offense when I read Rich Stearns of World Vision write about the apathy of the church regarding the rest of the world's needs in his bestseller, "The Hole in our Gospel." My mom worked hard to convince us kids how amazing it was to "get to, not have to" eat potato soup while we were sacrificing to send our pastor father on mission trips to India and Australia, or whenever we took some of the "mad money" change we were saving for vacation to dutifully share with the Annie Armstrong mission giving initiative instead.

"Where were you, Rich Stearns, when we were doing that? Getting your MBA at Wharton and pulling down big bucks as CEO at Lenox?" I shouted to the page, still triggered. "I'll tell you what a pastor's family in Festus, Missouri was doing. Eating potato soup and sleeping on the floor so missionaries could have our rooms!"

I know I was irrationally heated, and I know now I was missing his point. But you must understand, he was talking about my mother and me (not I) when he said the church in America didn't care." WE cared. I respect my mom for caring about world missions.

I respected her wisdom. I called my mom during my college years to tell her I was quitting and coming home. I was homesick and tired. School was hard and I worked at a part-time job I didn't like. Though I haven't heard her voice since the summer of 1983, when she died of a brain aneurysm, I can hear her voice as if she were saying it now: "Seems to me it'll be a lot easier if you stay there and finish than come home and try to explain why you didn't." I was left speechless at that prospect. I stayed.

I respected my mom for her one-liners. She was a queen of pithy, memorable sayings.

- *"Delight yourself in the Lord, and He will give you the desires of your heart."* (Psalm 37:4)

- *"Pretty is as pretty does.* Don't forget that."
- *"Be fun to live with!"* she told her Young Married Sunday School class as she concluded her lesson each week.
- *"Clean your plate."* This one we could have done without and has been a struggle. I threw it in to prove she wasn't perfect and to see if you were paying attention. :)
- *"You wouldn't worry so much about what people thought of you if you realized how little they did,"* is a well-worn cliché of hers that I know now is attributed to Eleanor Roosevelt. Mom, however, owned it like it originated with her.
- But by far, the simple three-word axiom my mother said to me that has shaped my life more than any other is this one—*"Money follows mission."* It bears repeating. Money. Follows. Mission.

In late May 1982, we were driving away from the campus of Dallas Theological Seminary when our conversation naturally turned to what we just experienced. That visit was the college graduation present I had asked for, and for my mother, driving back to her Texas roots was no sacrifice at all. She happily accommodated my request to visit a graduate school located in Dallas. Mom chose to love Missouri, but she couldn't hide her first love for the Lone Star State. Our visit to the campus included the customary tour of the facilities, a conversation with an admissions counselor, discussions about financial aid, and a multimedia slide show with two or more projectors and screens. When the Dallas Theological Seminary alumni and past/present professors were profiled, it was obvious Mom was impressed. And who wouldn't be? Norm Geisler, Charles Ryrie, John Walvoord, J. Dwight Pentecost, and of course, Prof (Howie Hendricks) were names she recognized and had even read some of their works.

An impromptu conversation we had with a couple of students outside the student center stood out to me. One claimed Presbyterian and the other was from the Bible church tribe. The seminary crossed denominational lines, and while it felt risky given our Baptistic roots, it appealed to me. I wasn't surprised my mom wasn't put off by it, but I knew in my gut it was a stretch for her to support it if it's what I wanted to do.

"So, what are you thinking? Do you want to apply?" she asked as our vehicle headed north for the long drive home.

"I want to go there," I said, giving voice to my soul racing with enthusiasm at the prospect. But just then I tempered my enthusiasm with a dose of reality. "But you know we can't afford it."

Her husband was dead. Her Social Security check was limited. Her vocation had been in the ministry, not in the marketplace. I didn't have any money, and I knew her funds to help were quite limited. In the moment, I felt proud of my pragmatism despite my longing for further equipping in theology at a respected graduate school like this one. To admit the obvious seemed completely justified. It was out of the question. Why bother considering it? We can't afford it.

I no sooner declared it than she responded. Her retort was swift and pointed, corrective to its core. "We don't talk like that. It's not the way our family lives. **Money follows mission!**" Without taking a breath, she went on, "Where God guides, He provides. Where He leads, He feeds. I don't ever want to hear you talk like that again. Do you hear me, young man? I mean it!"

This wasn't the Holy Spirit's voice in the way I've described it in the previous ten chapters. This time the power of the whisper was human and audible, yet equally impactful. With that correction and her instruction to just take the next step, I applied and received my acceptance letter only a few months later.

While I waited for my first semester to start, I worked as a night shift auditor, lived at home, and saved all I could. The financial gap was wide, but I dared not give vent to my financial fears where my mother might hear it. It's called faith for a reason. Things we hope for, not yet seen, Hebrews 11:1 teaches us. It is a confident expectation that if God is in it, we can have a firm conviction that He will make a way.

Who knew, but God, that it would be Mom's unexpected death that made the way financially for me to attend DTS full time and to do so without incurring any debt. In total, the estate we inherited from Mom and Dad, when settled and divided among the five kids, was $25,000. It was just enough to pay for the four-year tuition, an eight-week missions adventure to the Philippines, and a 30-day study trip in Israel through the Institute of Holy Land Studies. We moved to Columbia with $3,200 and used the remainder to purchase sound equipment for our new church start.

I hasten to add that I would rather have had access to my mom than have the money to further my education. But the irony in her correction becoming the means should not be missed. It is my conclusion that while God is in control, He is not controlling. There's not a reason for everything, yet all things work together for the good of those who love Him and are called according to His good purpose. I don't say God took my mom. Of course, He knew the number of her days. What a good gift we have in Providence. The mysteries of God's redemptive will make me want to worship Him. I look forward to seeing Mom again someday. I wonder if she'll pull me close and whisper in my ear, "I told you God would provide. See? Jesus never lets you down. Money follows mission!"

YOUR STORY

What adventure with God might you be squelching because you have predetermined you can't afford it? What longing is in you that builds others up and you find life-giving that you've concluded won't work since the resources are not readily available? What fears are keeping you from committing to giving it a go?

Come with me to consider the biblical account we find in the book of Joshua. The promised land, full of adventure and flourishing with God's provisions, is on the other side of the rushing waters. The next generation of Israelites are on this side of the swift river with an invitation to go and enjoy the good that awaits them. It won't be without sacrifice. There will be challenging circumstances ahead of the reward. But staying here wandering in the wilderness isn't easy either. They want to go home to a place with an abundance (flowing) of milk (cattle, agricultural necessities) and honey (figs and dates, luxury) where they live their best life. But they haven't yet set foot on that side of the river yet and there is a raging torrent of water between them and over there.

I have imagined myself with them on the banks of the Jordan time and again when considering this idea of how to risk with God. The generation whose parents had experienced freedom from slavery and all the miracles that accompanied that event had died. Moses was dead. Joshua had his instructions from God. The pep talk he received included what a coffee mug in your cabinet might have stamped on the front of it: "Have I not commanded you? **Be strong and courageous.** Do not be afraid; do not be discouraged, for the Lord your God will be with you wherever you go!" (Joshua 1:9)

A literal reading of this verse could be, "... when the feet of the priests had been **dipped** into the water's edge..." The question I like to ask is this, "What was going through the minds of the dudes who were ankle deep as the flood waters were bearing down ahead of them?" What did those seconds feel like? I wonder if the people in the back were like, "I told you this was a bad idea," or "Let's play it safe, make do with what we have and make the best of it. What'dya say?"

Check it out yourself for full impact in Joshua 3:7, 15-16. God had them pack their bags, put everything on their backs or in a cart, place the ark of the covenant on their shoulders, **and** wade in before the water stopped flowing. They were able to cross over. Sometimes with God, miracles don't happen without a requirement of risk. "But God," we argue, "If you will just make it clear that I won't be embarrassed, or disappoint my parents, and show me the money, and guarantee me I won't fail, then I'll do what you've put in my heart to do." We're unwilling to get our ankles wet.

I get it. One time I committed to going with a group of people to a conference in southern California. I wanted to see the church ministry model where the event was being held. It was a learning experience. I couldn't see any reason for not attending. Although

I didn't have the money, I was willing to risk it would come. It didn't. I was embarrassed when I called to tell them I couldn't go and why. I learned that day that flood waters don't always stop just because we step into them. That's why it's called taking a risk.

I illustrate this axiom like this: A+B+C+D=E. In my story, E equals being a student at Dallas Seminary. A is filling out an application. B is how I will spend the gap year before I go. C is how will it be paid for. And D is whatever courses I may be required to take as prerequisites before I can get in. The point my mom was making about the money was not to let C come before A. Do the next thing. Don't talk yourself out of an adventure because you don't have all the answers you want as a guarantee it'll all work out. Take that risk. Take the next step in faith.

1. What is it, even if you might fail, that has God put in your heart to do?
2. What are your thoughts about the idea that Jesus did not concern Himself with outcomes, but only whether He was doing His Father's will as He knew it.
3. Meditating on Joshua 3, where do you imagine yourself in their experience? As Joshua, or as a priest ankle deep in the water, or at the back of the line watching and waiting?
4. Is there an A step of faith you need to take? It'll be so good if you do.

CHAPTER TWELVE

"Take a day off."

─────

EVERY FAMILY FINDS THEMSELVES somewhere on the continuum of dysfunction. Every parent is navigating, to one degree or another, how they experience a lack of feeling seen, soothed, safe, and secure. We all need Jesus to fill the gap that only He can. Whether we label the gap mild, moderate, or acute, every human has stumbled when it comes to coping with life's stress.

Socially unacceptable coping mechanisms include self-indulgence, laziness, and unregulated outbursts of anger. More socially acceptable habits of handling stress that families employ include perfection, rescuing, and religion.

My parents coped with their own dysfunctional growing-up experiences through socially acceptable coping skills. There's a lot to celebrate about that. When they met Jesus as young adults, they were rightly overwhelmed by God's love and sacrificially participated in building His kingdom. But their sacrifices were too often unreasonable from my perspective and in this recounting, it's the one that matters. Their children paid a price.

Except for one meaningful conversation my father had with me, my default memory when I think of him was the back of his head disappearing through the back door of the church. I would be kicking a football or shooting hoops, wishing he would stop, but he never did. Dad was too busy saving souls and preparing sermons. You might think I'm exaggerating, but I'm not. My wife, who was a teenager in our church youth group, experienced more of a blessing from my father than I did. That ain't right.

Both parents were overworked. Mom was invested in cooking meals, painting flannelgraph, counseling women who were hurting, and treating bedsores for her bedridden mother. Dad prepared three sermons a week, built buildings for the church camp, visited the sick and shut-ins, and tended to a small farm outside of town, feeding 40 head of cattle and a hundred hogs. Amid the swirl was joy and enthusiasm that accompanied my parents' business. They didn't complain about the sheep they tended with Jesus. No one was making them do this. It was a privilege to be called a pastor and family. Whatever sacrifice came with it, this is the day the Lord has made. This embroidered framed artwork hung in our hallway as a constant reminder: *"Only one life will soon be past and only what's done for Christ will last."*

Neither my siblings nor I were accused of being lazy. My parents' work ethic remedied that. Workaholism runs in my family. Knowing my limits without doing harm to my body or my own family relationships was my biggest challenge. Even now, I must work at rest.

This gives you the context for the whisper I'm about to describe. I was sitting in Chafer Chapel on the campus of Dallas Seminary when I heard it. It was orientation week for incoming first-year students. I had moved to "the big D" a few weeks before and was looking for employment to supplement my financial needs. Only a few weeks earlier we had buried my mom from the aneurysm that snuffed out her physical life. My father died three years prior. There were mixed feelings of support from my siblings over my attending a school that didn't fly a Baptist flag. Back home in Missouri, my soon-to-be fiancée was teaching high school students. Even though DTS accepted me, I was placed on academic probation because my college grade point average fell below the 3.25 threshold the seminary required. To say I was a wreck but still ready to work is a gross understatement of the anxiety and grief I carried into the chapel service that afternoon.

The presenter that day was Don Sunukjian. I quickly discovered he was a student of Haddon Robinson, who was considered by many to be the guru of biblical preaching for our generation. Don had a Ph.D. in communication, had been the teaching pastor of Scottsdale Bible Church, only to return to DTS to train up the next generation of pastors. I took every class he taught in preaching and pastoral ministry. I studied Advanced Homiletics under his tutelage once again during my doctoral program at BIOLA University. As of this writing, Don still teaches there at the age of 85. His mentoring, though mostly from a distance, inspires me still. Don's homiletic (preaching) principles are a ministry philosophy I share. His winter-term course, "Persuasion in Preaching" is at the foundation of any contribution I've made to the field of preaching and teaching. Though I take full blame for any errors and do not insist Don endorse my applications, like it or not, his influence runs deep in my ministry veins.

Don's proposition that afternoon was crystal clear. His text was an application of one of the big 10 (commandments) precepts

Moses brought down from Mount Sinai. The text? "Remember the sabbath day and keep it holy." Don's translation? **"You will accomplish more in six days than in seven if you take a day off."** It rocked my world. Oh, the power of a big idea. Especially, a big idea from the pages of an ancient book embedded with timeless truths applied in clear and relevant language for contemporary hearers.

It was why I had come to study at Dallas Seminary. I was experiencing from Don the same thing I experienced when listening to "Insight for Living" with Chuck Swindoll. This was why I wanted to attend this seminary in the first place; I wanted to "learn the Bible and communicate it half as well." That was the way I put it back then. I felt convinced about the assertion that day in chapel, but for it to have any authority, I needed to apply it. The assertion that Don was making was foreign to me.

We pastor kids kept a sabbath of sorts, no question about that. There was lots of time spent at the church building. We didn't go out to eat or shop for groceries on Sunday because some restaurant or store employee might miss church because they had to work. One time in high school, I had to complete a theological debate with my mom before she finally released me to play basketball with friends at a public park. Between Training Union at 6 p.m. and our evening church service following, not to mention, youth choir practice at 4:30 p.m. most Sundays, there wasn't much time for fun anyway. Sunday School and lunch had to figure in also, as well as the dishes washed and laid out to dry. Suffice it to say, we had a sabbath, but it wasn't restful. We were tired.

The track this preacher was laying down that day was different. Don strongly suggested that Sundays were typically a day with expectations for the ministry crowd, and since that was the case, we would receive an unexpected gift from God if we picked a different day. We would get more done in six days than in seven if we protected our schedule by taking a day to chill. His instruction was practical and specific. As much as is humanly possible, Don proposed we wake up on that day and ask ourselves the question, *"What do I want to do today?"*

He went on to tell us how we would be tempted to study for an upcoming Greek quiz or get ahead in our required reading for a class. How was he able to read our minds? Don boldly encouraged us to resist the temptation. He challenged us to do our shopping on a workday, unless it was life-giving, which would be acceptable. Don asked us to trust God in the gap of our anxiety about not getting everything done. He cautioned us that it would take weeks before we would experience the full benefits of surrendering to the mysteries of the biblical invitation to rest. One day a week. Every week. I'm certain he mentioned sabbaticals, scheduling, family vacations, etc., but I don't recall any of that. I was still in shock and awed by the power of this proposition and the Spirit's whisper that accompanied it.

I made this commitment that day. Almost without exception, I have kept it, only violating it when a funeral or such demands. I've said repeatedly through the years, "If I finish my life without going bitter, other than marrying well, it'll be because I respected a day off."

Of course, various seasons of life insisted on various reiterations of what it meant to have a day off. On the days my wife was working a part-time job to help ends meet, I was responsible for the care of our two daughters. I quickly learned I needed to be creative. Yard sales and reading at the McDonald's Play Place became my regular routine in that season. Julie and I needed to negotiate her day off as best we could, given her multiple duties as a mom. My point is not that we nailed it. My point is that we cared about it. We worked at resting. We trusted God to make up the difference. We still do.

Those who know me know two things I value. One, I want to turn 73 (83, 93) and still be the life of the kingdom party. Two, I want to say yes to the following question: "Am I living the kind of life I can legitimately invite my children and grandchildren to join me in?"

If you resonate with either or both of those sentiments, take seriously the divine whisper I heard that day when a chapel speaker opened the text and called for a decision. "Take a day off. You will get more done in six than in seven if you do." It's one of the key ingredients to the sauce of a life well lived.

YOUR STORY

Early in the TV show's history, the "American Idol" champion would perform a song immediately after having been crowned. They called this song the winner's single. Imagine with me how different the contestant must have felt singing that song as opposed to all the other songs they performed during the competition. With those earlier songs, they tried to impress the judges and TV voters. When they sang the winner's song, however, they were free to express without fear of losing. It's a safe bet they felt more freedom, less anxiety, and a lot more joy, don't you think?

When we grow in our understanding of what we have in our union with Christ, we can attend to our kingdom work as freely as an "American Idol" winner. We are not striving *for* something; we are serving *from* something—that something that a Someone accomplished in His death, burial, and resurrection. It is no longer *my performance + other's approval = my identity*. We are who He says we are, His child. As I John 3:1 reminds us, *"See how very much our Father loves us, for he calls us his children, and that is what we are!"* I'm confident the Scripture teaches that we have one nature, not two. Since we were all born unattached from knowing the security of God's love and imperfectly nurtured by human adults, we live out unhealthy ways of coping. The Scripture calls these "flesh patterns." Self-justification, people-pleasing, avoiding, aggression, greed, hiding, and overwork are a few examples of the way sin's consequences may look in our lives. The struggle is real, but the power to make progress in the freedom we have is stronger. These motivations and behaviors are not who we are; they are how we have coped. Do you know who you are in Christ? A saint who sins, not a sinner who sometimes gets it right. I pray you will see it and never be able to unsee it. How you think about your identity is a game changer.

When we take a day each week to rest, invest in spiritual retreats, schedule multiweek sabbaticals, turn off our cell phones, and disappoint people because we tell them no, we are reminded there is a God, and we are not Him. These acts and other spiritual practices honor our limited capacity. They remind us of the truth that we are not what we do. We are not what is said about us. We don't have to hurry and there's no need to worry. Jesus is the king. We serve in His kingdom. Trust me, a day off will help you keep this straight.

If you struggle with lack of motivation for the work you are doing, then let's get help with that. If you hear me giving you permission to be a slacker and shirk your responsibility as a shepherd of God's flock, then I haven't communicated well. I will assume your posture is, "Can you believe I get to do this?" or "I would gladly pay for the privilege of pastoring you, if I could."

I appreciate the quote attributed to Charles Spurgeon in his "Letters to My Students": "Do not enter the ministry, if you can help it." We need women and men who want to serve our campuses, faith communities, and nonprofit ministries, not those looking to make a living or serve under compulsion. Of course, not every day in the service of our Lord is a holiday and every meal is not a banquet. Someone suggested ministry work can be compared to Noah's ark; the stench on the inside would be unbearable were it not for the alternative on the outside. Despite that, no one is making us do it. We keep choosing it.

If you want to make a change and seek out marketplace ministry, there's no shame in that. Instead, that's to be celebrated. That's ministry too! Every member of Christ's body is a minister. Though my focus in this season is primarily about coaching ministry leaders who are equipping others, I gave the first half of ministry in the field helping educators, politicians, financial advisors, and laborers fulfill the common good where they were. The goal is to be fully present where you are, pursuing a flourishing life, living the gospel, wherever that may be.

Growing into our identity in Christ takes time. We have it, but experiencing the fullness of it is a process. It's like a little boy wearing his father's dress shirt. He grows into it, until one day, it fits. Or another way of putting it—it is like being married. You're as married on the first day as you are ever going to ever be, but after 40-plus years of honoring and submitting to one another under God, you come to experience your identity as a married person more fully.

So, whatta ya' say? Stop struggling to be good. Rest in the fact that you are good to struggle. Stop thinking your way into a new way of living and live your way into a new way of thinking. Take a day off.

1. Is it hard for you to think about taking time off to recreate? Why or why not?
2. How do you still struggle with thinking you are only as valuable as what you do, have, or what people think of you?
3. Watch "The Path" videos by Trueface Ministries on YouTube for more on our union with Christ. Check out their website at Trueface.org.
4. Spend time ingesting and digesting the following:
   - John 1:12—I am God's child.
   - John 15:15—As a disciple, I am a friend of Jesus Christ.
   - I Corinthians 6:17—I am united with the Lord, and I am one with Him in spirit.
   - 1 Corinthians 6:19&20—I have been bought with a price, and I belong to God.

- Ephesians 1:3-8—I have been chosen by God and adopted as His child.
- Colossians 2:9,10—I am complete in Christ.
- Hebrews 4:14-16—I have direct access to the throne of grace through Jesus Christ.
- Romans 8:28—I am assured that God works for my good in all circumstances.

Afterword

I T SEEMS FITTING to conclude the accounting of my unexpected journey of divine whispers with an account of where more of my spiritual life has been lived. In this story, there's been no power of a whisper as distinct as the ones I describe in these 12 chapters. Resilience and grit are the primary elements needed then. Pruning is an apt descriptor of what we experience during these seasons. "Where would we go, you (Jesus) have the words of life" (John 6:67-69) is sometimes the only thing keeping us from quitting and singing along with the classic, "I did it MY WAY." There are provisions for sure, but they come in small bites; just enough to get you through the day. Or perhaps better said, just enough to get you through the long nights when you can't go to sleep ... or when you go to sleep and wake up almost wishing you hadn't.

In these seasons of suffering, we want things to make sense. We want to know if there's a reason for everything, and if there is, what's the reason for what we're enduring now. We ask for a divine word. A sentence. Or a sign. But heaven seems silent. And we wonder, having followed Jesus as best we knew how, was it worth it? Here's an accounting of one of those seasons.

"The question I hear you asking is this ..." said my counselor: **"Was it worth it?"** When I heard Dr. Call ask it, I began to cry ... sob really ... the ugly, "I can't control myself though I'm trying to" kind of wailing. Even as I write about that session, I feel my body react. My breathing grows shallow, and my brain fades as a fog sets in. The loneliness I was experiencing and the anger surfacing with it was affecting my marriage and my wife, Julie, **insisted** I see someone professionally. The brutal truth of no longer being a part of, nor feeling welcome in a faith community that my family and I had faithfully served for two decades wasn't fading, and the well-intentioned advice of others to "just move on" wasn't working.

The hardest season

I was serving as an associate pastor and member of a five-person leadership team in an evangelistically effective ministry that valued both relevance and discipleship. Foolishly, the governing body prematurely reinstated the senior pastor who was admittedly guilty of violating pastoral ethics. His actions included traveling to conferences with younger single women and inappropriate bantering by text. A backdrop to his disciplinary "time out" prior to his reinstatement included ill-advised Facebook posts and time spent "pastoring" certain women—two examples of the unnecessary hurt his black-sheep reputation created for this revitalizing Baptist church. He was sidelined for only six months with a professional diagnosis of narcissism, histrionics, attention-seeking behavior, and rebellion, and many who benefitted from his gifted teaching (along with some uninformed staff) clamored for his reinstatement as lead pastor. I, along with others, predicted he wasn't ready, and his return would spell ruin for him and the faith community. (It did. Six months later with yet more misconduct, he was gone.)

"You're not ready," I told him. "You don't meet the qualifications of a ruling elder. Not yet. Namely," I continued, "you're not 'above reproach' and you don't possess 'a good reputation among outsiders.' It's also not good for you or your family, nor for me or mine," I insisted. "And know this," I concluded, "The day before your first day reinstated as senior pastor will be my last day identifying as a pastor here."

Despite my pleas to him, the staff, and the church's governing body, he was reinstated just days later, and my resignation read as follows:

> I won't be part of a system that reinstates the authority of a senior pastor who has hurt the sheep in the way that (name withheld) has. I confronted and protected him for 21 years about the issue, and four months is not enough time to have confidence of changes necessary to reinstate him as senior pastor.
>
> It is my perspective that the biblical qualifications of a church elder (Senior Pastor) responsible for vision and spiritual direction as mandated in I Timothy 3 and Titus 1 are not justified in light of the weight of evidence this past season has revealed.
>
> Having heard your decision to reinstate, I humbly submit this letter of resignation.

The dreaded NDA

Following my voluntary stepping down, the offer of three months' severance was gracious, but the **non-disclosure agreement** insisting "neither my spouse nor I discuss the circumstances leading up to nor the reasons for our resignation" that came with it wasn't. We refused to sign, in case you are wondering.

To say this ending to a two-decade ministry investment was painful is obvious. Eight more staff resignations followed mine. The decision, for all practical purposes, split the church. There was no "goodbye associate pastor and family, and thank you for your faithful service" party. My family suffered and their faith community no longer felt safe. We didn't move and the reminders of this too common story are still frequent as we navigate doctor visits and grocery store aisles.

The above account is a "Reader's Digest" version of circumstances that led to the emotional meltdown I described above when the professional therapist asked, "Was it worth it?" I was questioning the sacrifices made to see people far from God become passionate followers of the ways of Jesus.

The reduced compensation of being paid 65–70% of the senior pastor's salary despite having more education and working every bit as hard or harder. Was it worth it?

Hearing that the young couple my spouse and I invested six months of premarital counseling in were now attending a church down the street. Was it worth it?

Knowing that key volunteers joined the tribe now known as "nones." Was it worth it?

Hearing a parishioner say they are mad at you because "they expected the senior pastor to act like a teenager but needed you to be the adult." Was it worth it?

We come into vocational ministry (and life with God in general) with theological knowledge that recognition and reward are at God's discretion for God's purposes. The foundation of our faith includes crucifixes and times when we acknowledge evil wins. Outcomes do not determine the validity of fruitfulness. Our Leader did not let outcomes decide His responses. Whether God leads us or lets us, He uses it for good. All true, but these phrases and more are the fodder of religious jargon, pastoral ministry courses and conferences. I found the lived experience more challenging than theory.

When the hooey hit the fan

When the "hooey" hit the fan, a shame spiral ensued. I felt embarrassed, guilty, and inadequate to know what to do when my boss's actions created chaos. It was complicated by *a before the days of #metoo/#churchtoo* to know *#whatto* do. My part in the earlier years was to caution him, get him to agree to some typical boundaries, defend him to parishioners as being unaware of professional expectations, and be sure that each time his boss/ the board knew what I knew. Until I didn't. My growing fear that what did happen was going to happen along with my hopelessness that nothing could change justified my "I'm done" defending or discussing his professional violations. The available evidence of his behavior wasn't egregious enough to clearly demand his termination (though in retrospect, I think it was) and his response when confronted was remorse and a resolve to do better.

Given my disappointment that his superiors (the church board) were asking me what ought to be done with the problem of his tarnishing reputation, I lacked the foresight to keep the responsibility theirs and quietly lost hope in change. With this impending crisis looming, as an introvert with an avoidant attachment, I isolated and withdrew. I mean that previous sentence as an explanation not an excuse. When another incident occurred involving a husband threatening the senior pastor if he ever texted his wife again, I announced to him and my peers that I was done defending his supposed naivete, trying to solve the problem, and privately hoped for his resignation or evidence of scandal sufficient for his termination.

At the bottom rung of the shame spiral staircase was a severe anxiety rooted in "small t" traumas. These came from my younger-self experiences growing up in a parsonage, watching the dismantling of my home church as it was wrecked by a sexual scandal of an assistant pastor to my dad. In retrospect, I have an empathy for the disappointment of those who couldn't understand why someone as capable as I had been at leading through other crises was unwilling and unable to "fix" this latest crisis. Some key ministry volunteers blew the whistle that our lead shepherd was taking advantage of sheep entrusted to his care. Of course, they wouldn't understand my reactions. I didn't understand my reactions at the time. I only knew I was mad. I knew I didn't know what to do. I knew I wanted his selfish distractions to our mission to stop. I knew I felt alone. I felt misunderstood. But mostly, I was numb.

What I'm writing in this next paragraph isn't rational and not what I actually believe, but it is an attempt to give words to a deep wrestling happening inside me during that season. I repeat: What I'm about to say is what I found myself wishing were true because the reality of what was actually true felt unbearable. I wanted to convert to Catholicism, or become a proponent of liturgy, or go to law school in my mid-50s. My gut wanted a clean break from what had been. I wanted to say employing a culturally engaged, less-assumptive, creative strategy was flawed. I now see the light, and what I should have given the first half of my ministry life to was better found anywhere outside the contemporary, mega-church world I was invested in. The "I made a youthful mistake, and I now see the light" approach felt easier than reality. And that reality is a confidence in the theological and missiological foundations undergirding the strategy we employed. The problem wasn't the approach, nor was the solution to be found in a different denomination. The fact remained, the outcome was worse than a pizza with no cheese, and there wasn't a dadgum thing I could do to change it.

Our Daily Bread
The big idea of this piece is not primarily to encourage the resources that were helpful, as helpful as those things were (and are.) It's that God provides "daily bread," and I keep saying yes. As important as it was to KNOW that recognition and reward are at God's discretion and for God's purposes, and it mattered that I COMMITTED with my peers to finish well, my take is that when "the snot got knocked out of us," it was TRUST in God providing daily bread that keeps me concluding **it was worth it!**

This little phrase from the model prayer of Jesus is gold to me now. I pray it daily. I refer to it often in conversation. "Father, give us this day our daily bread." I don't know what I need. I don't have what it takes to not go bitter. I can't discern that fine line between the disgust I feel and the unforgiveness you forbid. I'm embarrassed that my mind races and my body faints when I encounter a former board member who with others made a costly decision to reinstate the perpetrator and authorize a non-disclosure agreement. "Lord, give me this day the sustenance necessary (daily bread) to not conclude it wasn't worth it."

What daily bread looks like

Of course, the daily bread I need comes in a variety of shapes, sizes, and flours. Just like there's bagel choices that include asiago cheese and pumpernickel, there are podcasts and books. While bread comes baked like ciabatta or fried like tortilla chips, daily bread for me in my hardest season came in forms that are universally recognized as essential. Continuing to tell my story more authentically and making peace with how it shapes me was crucial in every season. My spouse is the most capable mentor I know. Her questions, coaching, and modeling are my greatest assets. My children cheered me on and reminded me it was more than okay to be human. Lanny, Scott, and Steve were therapy professionals I needed. They plowed the soil of my story and planted some seeds my soul needed. 1John , 2John, 3John (not the Bible books, but the order in which I came to know these ministry partners), Scott, and Jed are ministry peers that met/meet every Thursday morning and listen with empathy as we resolve to not "shove it where the sun don't shine" like I'm tempted to do, particularly during the three years that included the events described. God used all these resources and more to keep me on the operating table until some good work He had planned for me was completed.

Other resources include Immanuel journaling, embracing any emotion, and cheering MIZZOU football. All these resources and more are gifts God provided me to live through that hardest season and tools I still use to stay healthy.

But the point of this chapter is not to recount those resources, as essential as they were. They can be found quite easily if you are willing to engage them, as hard or expensive as some of them may be. The point of this piece is to explain how God showed up in unexpected ways, and to witness that my heavenly Father was with me and His provisions to sustain me were what I needed, because He intimately knows me.

Was it worthless?
Let me conclude these musings by recounting a "bagel bite" of daily bread Heavenly Father gave recently. I was walking through the room when I overheard my adult daughter say a phrase to her mother in a conversation in which I wasn't participating. The comment wasn't said in my presence. I don't know the context in which it was said. It doesn't matter. But when I heard it, I had a spiritual encounter. I'm still digesting it like manna and its nourishment is sustaining me. I know without a doubt God gave it as He has done so many times before to keep me tender, surrendered, and keeping the faith. What I overheard her say was this: "Was it worth it? It wasn't worth less." Not worthless. Worth less. What's the difference, you ask? Worthless has a performative value. Did the benefits outweigh the costs? Worth less signals a relational value. It validates my motivations on my better days

when I pastored from a heart of love. Worth less reminds me of the heart of the Father who called and invited me into this pastoral life. The value of greater intimacy with God is of inestimable worth. It wasn't worth less even when I doubt if it was worth it.

Putting a value on the worthiness of the lived experience that service with God asks remains more interrogative than declarative. Was it worth it? It depends on the day or time of day you ask. Don't get me wrong, I live in a great house and probably have enough income to last for this lifetime, maybe. The work we do through our resource center allows us to be the mentors we always wished we'd had and work at a pace that's appropriate for the age that we are. In short, life is very good. While outcomes that include institutional stability, a retirement party, or a published best seller would be awesome, it's not looking like those things are in the cards for me. I do know the benefits of a good reputation and the gratitude of some for the hours of pastoral counseling or a sermon that changed the trajectory of their life. Ministry wasn't worthless. But the loneliness leading to despair that landed me in that therapy session where Steve asked, "Was it worth it?" still finds me grieving the losses described above. What is more certain after walking through the hardest season is **it wasn't worth less**.

When I consider the implications of the phrase, it wasn't worth less, I *know* now the freedom of words that used to allude me. Words like *I don't know, I feel disgusted, I need help,* or *I don't have the capacity to do that.* I now know how His strength is made perfect in my weakness. I'm gentle with me now when I can't do anything but nod when I bump into a former staff member who I let make me responsible for the chaos others created. Without minimizing the sacrifice our Leader made in His sacrifice, which invites our sacrifice for others, it wasn't worth less because His daily bread is Himself. I *know* now I'm not alone. I never was. These words come to mind from my playlist aptly titled "Soul Cry" and sung by the incomparable Whitney Houston.

My levees are broken
My walls have come crumbling down on me
The rain is falling
Defeat is calling
I need you to set me free
As I lay me down
Heaven, hear me now
Who on earth can I turn to?
I look to You (Oh Lord)
After all my strength is gone
In You, I can be strong
I look to You
And when melodies are gone
In You, I hear a song
I look to You[1]

Let me now ask you ...
Is it worth it? When you see others do bad and seem to flourish. Is it worth it?
Is it worth it? When you serve sacrificially and struggle to buy groceries. Is it worth it?
Is it worth it? A relative of yours acts like a heathen and other family members cater. You speak up to address the bad behavior and you get verbally accosted. Is it worth it?
Is it worth it? You show up for work on time. Is it worth it?

1   "I Look to You" lyrics. Universal Music Publishing Group. Robert S. Kelly.

You say your prayers at night. Is it worth it? You keep your promises. Is it worth it?

Was it worth it? Our Example lived a life without sin. Was it worth it?
Our Example didn't have a place to call his own. Was it worth it?
Our Example was betrayed by a friend named Judas. Was it worth it?
He was wrongly accused of treason and tried without a jury. Was it worth it?
He was beaten, mocked, and died a cruel death on a cross. Was it worth it?
His so-called best friends ran. Thomas left the country to hide. Was it worth it?
His body lay in a cold tomb and His spirit was at rest. Was it worth it?
He rose from the dead. Was it worth it?
He saved us from a meaningless life. Was it worth it?

He promised to return. Will it be worth it?
He asked us to be faithful with our part regardless of our circumstances. Will it be worth it?
He told us it wouldn't be easy. That we might not get the blessing of father, mother, and siblings. Will it be worth it?
He said this world isn't our final home and that He is preparing mansions for us to live in. Will it be worth it?
For those who don't quit, who stay tender, who run their race, we will hear Him say "Well done, thou good and faithful servant. Enter into the joy of the Lord."
Will it be worth it? There is a great cloud of witnesses cheering us on from the balcony of heaven. They want us to finish well. Will it be worth it?

It isn't worth less.

Remember the story I shared in another chapter about wanting to quit? As a college student, I called my mom and announced, "I'm coming home. I'm going to quit."

And she said, "Honey, you can do that, but it seems to me it'd be a lot easier for you to stay there and finish, than to come home and explain to the folks here at home why you didn't." I stayed.

Today? Same struggle, different day. I'm still tempted to quit. I still have doubts, but what am I going to do? I have decided to follow Jesus. No turning back. I guess I'll stay the course, hope for some whispers along the way, and keep the faith. It'll be easier than trying to explain why I didn't.

What are you going to do?

I have fought the good fight, I have finished the race, and I have remained faithful. And now the prize awaits me—the crown of righteousness, which the Lord, the righteous Judge, will give me on the day of his return. And the prize is not just for me but for all who eagerly look forward to his appearing. (2 Timothy 4:7-8, NLT)

Acknowledgements

I once read, in a source I can no longer locate, an illustration that went like this:

When she was in her early 20s, a young woman gave her father a simple, leather-bound journal. "Write anything," she said. "Stories from your life, things you've learned ... whatever you want me to know someday." He smiled, hugged her, and tucked it onto a shelf in his study.

Years passed. Life got full—family gatherings, long talks, quiet days together. And then, as life does, things changed. He grew sick, and eventually, he passed away. In the quiet days after the funeral, she found the journal again while going through his things. It looked untouched. No pages ruffled. No signs of writing. Her heart sank. Had he forgotten?

But when she opened the cover, there it was—just one line, handwritten in his familiar style: "Everything worthwhile I did, I learned from your mother. Get to know her." That was it. No chapters, no stories. Just that sentence, but somehow, it said everything.

Other than Jesus, Julie is the best thing that ever happened to me. The only girl I ever loved. The only one I've ever kissed. The same girl who took my breath the first time I saw her at the age of 14. Somebody asked me if she was co-writing this book with me. I was stumped as to how to answer. The answer is yes; her fingerprints are on every page.

My daughters Miriam and Hannah are mentors of mine, both in their youth and now in adulthood. I wish I had been the parent they are to their children. I wish I had been as relationally present to others as they are to those they serve. On top of all that, they married godly men, and they have kids (our grandkids) who I do things for that I wouldn't do for anyone else.

Scott Mitchell and John Gillman were cheerleaders of this project and readers who gave priceless feedback. Trust me, it's a much better read because of them.

Our financial supporters are indeed a gift that keeps on giving. When neighbors ask me if I'm retired, I ask them if their definition of retirement is getting to do what you love? When they say yes, I explain, "Well then, I guess we are. We get to do what we love to do at a pace that is appropriate to the age that we are." That's not possible without the monthly and special investments of those who give to Reliant Mission and/or TEI to sustain us financially. Like the women (and presumably men) recorded by Luke (8:1-3), they travel with us in fulfilling our part in this kingdom adventure. We couldn't do it without them, nor would we want to. Thank you!

To Fred Parry and the Carriage House team: I'm deeply grateful for your partnership in this endeavor. You did more than publish a book. You published a dream.

And finally, to the faith communities that exist in Festus, Missouri; Chattanooga, Tennessee; Gadsden, Alabama; East Dallas, Texas; and Central Missouri: You each played a role in entrusting me with pastoral responsibilities long before I was mature enough for the task. You are the collective body of Christ who modeled to me what it means to "keep the faith!"

"I have fought the good fight, I have finished the race, I have kept the faith." (2 Timothy 4:7-8) This is my life's verse. May it be so.

Immanuel Journaling

———

HERE IS A PRACTICE that I have found helpful in the last few years called Immanuel Journaling. The assumption behind the exercise is that God is always present and active. This journaling experience is a resource that helps me discover what is implicit (deep inside me) and make it explicit (bring it to the surface). It is an intersection of several disciplines including spiritual formation, emotional awareness, and neuroscience. You can read more about this practice here: *Joyful Journey: Listening to Immanuel* by E. James Wilder, Anna Kang, John and Sungshim Loppnow ©2015. Or visit LifeModelWorks.org for more application. Below is a modified version of the exercise as I was taught the tool (DeeperWalk.com) and how I use it in my journaling practice.

In your journaling, write your responses to these prompts with the assumption that God is speaking.

1. **I see you ...**
2. **I hear you ...**
3. **I know you ...**
4. **I am strong enough to ...**
5. **I am (en)abling you to ...**

Here's a living example:

08/06/2025

Good morning, Rod,

I see you ... sitting behind your computer staring out the window writing about your spiritual journey and wondering if it will ever become a book that people read.

I hear you ... voicing your disappointment that one acquisitions editor has already rejected your proposal and your waiting to hear from two others is taking so long. You are also wondering if self-publishing is the better route anyway. I also hear you wondering if your intentions for writing about these experiences will be misunderstood and you worry about the backlash you may receive.

I know you ... want to use your experiences and God-given wisdom to encourage and motivate next-generation ministry leaders. I know you want your children and their children to keep the faith and not give up on Me. You want them to bet their lives on the fact that I am a God who is with them (Immanuel).

I am strong enough ... to fulfill my purposes for what you have written. Take confidence, my son, I am the one who has compelled you to write. I am with you every step of this process. I can redeem whatever comes our way.

I am (en)abling you ... to finish this appendix. I am enabling you to wait on the readers to give you feedback. I am enabling you to reread and rewrite the final draft. I am enabling you to trust Me, Rod, again. "I, who have begun a good work in you, will be faithful to complete it."

* * *

My theological method is described as anabaptist. Our *experiences*, including hearing from God, is always subject to the interpretation of the *Scriptures* as our primary source of revelation. Sound *reasoning*, involving physics, logic, common sense, etc., also should inform our conclusions. Another source we consult are the church traditions—those concepts which Christians before us have concluded to be true. As anabaptists, we hold this one at arm's length and consider it with an eye of skepticism given a history of persecution for things like refusing to baptize infants. A respect for the priesthood of all believers is another distinction of our method for doing theology. On its best days, the proper conclusion of this *community* resource is not isolation, but consensus.

It is imperative that this journaling practice not live in isolation. Together we submit our lives to the Bible, good reason, shared experiences, and church tradition to conclude what is God's will for us. In other words, summaries of the thoughts that surface in our Immanuel Journaling encounters need to be shared in your community of believers. Spiritual friends help us discern the ways and work of God in our lives. The power of your whispers is best discerned and lived out together. For together there is great hope!

"...be strong in the grace that is in Christ Jesus. And the things you have heard me say in the presence of many witnesses entrust to reliable people who will also be qualified to teach others." — 2 Timothy 2:1-2 (NIV)

Partner with us.

The mission of the Theological Education Initiative is to sustain healthier faith communities through providing theological, philosophical, and practical resources for next-generation ministry leaders.

If you have found this resource helpful, would you prayerfully consider investing with us by giving a financial gift? Together we can continue to provide lifelong learning for under-resourced church, campus, and nonprofit leaders.

Your investment makes possible:
A Christian Study Center with a theological reference library
Tuition assistance for continuing education
Visiting scholars for lectures and seminars
The Emerging Church Leadership Institute (ECLI)

Ways to Give
Online: teimissouri.org/donations
By Mail: TEI, 601 Business Loop 70W, Columbia, MO 65203
By Text: 573-285-0159

Thank you for sharing in this calling. I am deeply grateful for your prayers, your generosity, and your partnership on this journey.

Keeping the faith with you,
rod

You can support us in our mission to equip church and campus ministry leaders.

SCAN THE QR CODE TO DONATE!

601 W Business Loop 70, Ste 131, Columbia, MO 65203
office@teimissouri.org

Dr. Rod Casey is passionate about equipping next-generation ministry leaders. He is the director of the Theological Education Initiative (TEI), teimissouri.org, a Christian Study Center serving the theologically under-resourced in Central Missouri. After more than three decades in pastoral ministry, he and his wife now serve as the mentors they wish they'd had. Rod is a graduate of Dallas Theological Seminary and earned a Doctor of Ministry degree from Talbot School of Theology. In addition to his mentoring, he teaches preaching and writes for *Preaching* magazine and "Preaching Today." He is married to his high school sweetheart, Julie. She cares about emotionally healthy spirituality and coming alongside women needing healing from the pain of their stories. They have four grandchildren they adore and enjoy spending time with their two daughters and their husbands. Rod lives under the illusion that with better coaching he could have played in the NBA.

* * *